Factory Reset Your Dopamine

The 30-Day Protocol toStop Wasting Your Life, Overcome Addiction, and Restore Motivation

Andy Skinner

© Copyright 2025 – Andy Skinner – All rights reserved

The content within this book may not be reproduced, duplicated, or transmitted without direct written permission from the author or the publisher.

Under no circumstances will any blame or legal responsibility be held against the publisher, or author, for any damages, reparation, or monetary loss due to the information contained within this book, either directly or indirectly.

Legal Notice

This book is copyright protected. This book is only for personal use. You cannot amend, distribute, sell, use, quote, or paraphrase any part, or the content within this book, without the consent of the author-publisher.

Disclaimer Notice

Please note that the information contained within this document is for educational and entertainment purposes only. All effort has been executed to present accurate, up-to-date, and reliable, complete information. No warranties of any kind are declared or implied. Readers acknowledge that the author is not engaging in the rendering of legal, financial, medical, or professional advice.

Table of Content

About Me and Why I Wrote This Book 6

Chapter 1: The Dopamine Trap 8

    Why You Can't Focus Anymore 8

    The Neuroscience of Digital Hijacking 10

    How Your Brain Became a Pleasure Junkie 12

    The Real Cost of Instant Gratification 14

    The Candy vs Vegetables Effect 16

Chapter 2: Diagnosing Your Addiction 19

    Quick Self-Check: Early Warning Signs 20

    The Four Types of Modern Addiction 21

    Your Personal Stimulation Audit 24

    When Fun Becomes Dysfunction 27

    The Seven Symptoms Checklist 29

Chapter 3: The Myth of Willpower 34

    Why You Keep Failing to Change 35

    Environment Beats Motivation Every Time 36

    The Depletion Trap 38

    Building Systems Instead of Resolutions 40

    Brain Chemistry vs Character Flaws 43

Chapter 4: Preparing For The Reset 45

    Setting Your Baseline and Goals 45

    Identifying Your Biggest Triggers 48

    Creating Your Detox Blueprint 51

    Building Your Support System 54

    The Replacement Strategy 57

Chapter 5: The 30-day Dopamine detox 61

    Days 1-2: The Discomfort Phase 62

Days 3-7: Breaking Point and Breakthrough 64

Days 8-14: Rebuilding Reward Pathways 67

Days 15-21: Momentum Building 71

Days 22-30: Integration and Testing 74

A Minute That Makes a Difference 77

Chapter 6: Reclaiming Your Focus **78**

The Art of Deep Work 78

Training Your Attention Span 81

Mastering Monotasking 84

Building Your Concentration Muscle 87

The Morning 90-Minute Rule 90

Chapter 7: Rebuilding Real Motivation **94**

Discovering Intrinsic vs Extrinsic Drive 94

Creating Meaningful Goals That Pull You Forward 97

The Power of Micro-Progress 99

Celebrating Without Relapsing 101

From Forcing to Flowing 103

Chapter 8: Managing Relapses and Urges **106**

Understanding the Relapse Cycle 106

Your Emergency Response Toolkit 109

The 10-Minute Rule 111

Turning Setbacks Into Comebacks 114

Sitting With Discomfort 116

Chapter 9: Designing Your New Life **120**

Replacing Old Habits With Better Ones 121

Curating Your Digital Environment 123

Building Offline Rituals 125

Finding Flow in Ordinary Activities 126

Phone Boundaries That Actually Work 128

Chapter 10: The Long Game 131

    Tracking What Matters Long-Term 132

    The Quarterly Audit 133

    Adapting to Life Changes 136

    Building Antifragile Systems 138

    When to Reset Again 141

Chapter 11: Beyond Yourself 144

    The Contribution Paradox 145

    Finding Your Service 147

    Teaching What You've Learned 150

    Creating Systems for Others 152

    The Ripple Effect 154

Chapter 12: Living Awake 157

    What Nobody Tells You 157

    The Inverse Relationship 160

    Resistance Is Information 163

    Permission to Disappoint... 166

    What You're Actually Building.. 168

Help Someone Find Their Focus.. 171

Final Words.. 172

Bibliography.. 174

About Me and Why I Wrote This Book

I was standing in my kitchen at two in the morning, phone in hand, scrolling through nothing. I'd opened Twitter to check one thing and forty minutes had disappeared. Arguments between strangers about topics I didn't care about while my coffee went cold. When I looked up, I felt hollow. Drained. I did the math: two to three hours daily lost to this pattern. Almost a thousand hours a year, gone, for absolutely nothing I could name.

I wasn't always like this. I remember being a kid who could read for six hours straight. Who could build something all Saturday and lose track of time. By thirty, I couldn't read a book anymore. Not "didn't read." Couldn't. Three pages and my mind would drift, thinking about checking my phone.

I'm a writer by trade. But all I had were five-minute bursts between distractions. I started projects I couldn't finish. Made commitments I couldn't keep. Present physically but absent mentally in every conversation, every moment. I tried everything. Productivity books. App deletions. Website blockers I'd override within hours. Nothing worked, or it would work for a week then I'd slide back.

Then I found research on dopamine. Not the pop science version, but the real mechanism: how the system could be hijacked. After years of high-stimulation digital content, my brain had adapted. Normal activities couldn't compete anymore. They weren't stimulating enough.

This wasn't willpower. This was biology. My attention system was dysregulated at the neurochemical level. I designed a reset protocol. Thirty days. Complete elimination of the highest-stimulation activities. No social media, streaming, news sites, games.

The first days were hell. Physically uncomfortable. By day five, worse:

flatness. Nothing felt interesting.

Around day twelve, something shifted. I was reading and realized I'd been focused for thirty minutes without looking up. Just reading, present, satisfied. That sounds small. It felt huge. For the first time in years, I could hold my attention on one thing.

I've done four resets since then. I'm not cured. I still have hard days. But I have tools now. I understand what's happening. I can course-correct before complete regression.

More importantly, I'm present in my life now. I show up fully. I complete projects. My relationships are deeper. My work is better.

Not because I'm special. Because I understood the problem correctly and applied solutions that actually addressed it.

So why this book?

When I was struggling, I couldn't find what I needed. Productivity advice assumed functioning attention. Addiction literature was too extreme. Neuroscience was too vague.

I needed someone to explain exactly what was happening and what specific steps would reset the system. Practical protocols. Honesty about the difficulty.

Nobody had written that. So I did.

I'm not an expert or neuroscientist. I'm someone who struggled, studied obsessively, experimented, and found what worked.

If you recognize something in what I've described—if your attention isn't what it used to be, if you spend hours on your phone and can't remember why, if you're living half-present—this book is for you.

Not because I have all the answers. Because I've walked this path and can show you what it looks like. The journey isn't easy. But it's possible. And what you gain is worth every uncomfortable moment.

Let's begin.

Chapter 1:
The Dopamine Trap

"The things you own end up owning you." — Chuck Palahniuk

Imagine your brain as a smartphone with 47 apps running simultaneously in the background. The battery drains faster than you can charge it. Everything lags. Simple tasks take forever. You keep restarting the device, but nothing helps.

That's exactly what's happening inside your skull right now.

Three years ago, I was that guy checking his phone every thirty seconds. Starting projects but never finishing them. Sitting at my desk for eight hours but accomplishing maybe ninety minutes of real work. My brain felt like it was stuck in molasses—slow, heavy, resistant to every task that mattered.

I thought I was lazy. I thought I lacked discipline. I downloaded every productivity app, watched hundreds of motivational videos, tried meditation apps that collected digital dust after three days.

Nothing worked.

Then I discovered something that changed everything: I wasn't broken. My dopamine system had been hijacked.

This chapter isn't about scaring you. It's about showing you what's really happening in your brain when you can't focus, can't finish what you start, and can't seem to feel satisfied by anything anymore. Once you understand the trap, you can escape it.

Why You Can't Focus Anymore

Let's start with a simple question: When was the last time you read a book for two hours straight without checking your phone?

If you can't remember, you're not alone. And you're not broken.

Your brain wasn't designed for the world we live in. Our ancestors' reward systems evolved over hundreds of thousands of years to respond to things like finding food, connecting with their tribe, or accomplishing difficult tasks. These rewards were scarce and hard-won, which made them valuable.

> **Quick stat**
> The average smartphone user taps, swipes, or clicks their device about 2,600 times a day—and heavy users exceed 5,400 interactions daily. (Dscout Mobile Touch Study, 2016)

Fast forward to today. You wake up, and within thirty seconds, your brain gets more stimulation than your great-grandfather experienced in a month. Every notification is a tiny reward. Every like is a small win. Every new video is a fresh hit of novelty.

Your brain releases dopamine—the "motivation molecule"—in response to these rewards. But here's where it gets dangerous: your brain adapts.

Think about the last time you walked into a room with a strong smell. Maybe fresh paint or someone's perfume. Within minutes, you stop noticing it. Your nose didn't break. It adapted. It decided that smell wasn't important anymore and filtered it out.

Your dopamine system does the same thing.

When you flood your brain with constant micro-rewards, it starts turning down the volume on its dopamine receptors. It's protecting itself from overstimulation. But this creates a vicious cycle: now you need more stimulation to feel the same level of reward.

This is why reading a book feels boring. Why having a conversation without checking your phone feels impossible. Why working on that important project feels like pushing a boulder uphill.

The activities themselves haven't changed. Your brain's ability to find reward in them has been systematically destroyed.

I learned this the hard way. I remember sitting in a strategy meeting with my business partner, supposedly discussing a project that could change everything for us. Twenty minutes in, I realized I hadn't heard a word he'd said. My hand was in my pocket, fingers wrapped around my phone, itching to check if anyone had texted me.

Nothing important was happening on my phone. I knew that. But my brain didn't care. It had been trained to expect a dopamine hit every few minutes, and it was throwing a tantrum because it wasn't getting one.

That's when I realized: I wasn't present in my own life anymore. I was just a passenger, watching my attention get stolen by whatever app had the best algorithm.

The scariest part? Most people don't even notice it's happening. They just think they're getting older, or stressed, or naturally losing their edge. They blame themselves for lacking willpower when the real problem is neurological.

Your focus isn't gone. It's just buried under years of digital overstimulation.

The Neuroscience of Digital Hijacking

Here's something they don't teach you in school: every app on your phone was designed by teams of neuroscientists and behavioral psychologists whose job is to hack your brain.

I'm not exaggerating. Social media companies spend billions of dollars studying how to trigger dopamine release in your brain. They run thousands of experiments to figure out exactly which notification sounds, which colors, which features will keep you scrolling longest.

Instagram's red notification badge? Carefully chosen to trigger urgency. TikTok's endless scroll? Designed to mimic the variable reward schedule that makes slot machines so addictive. YouTube's autoplay? Built to override your intention to "just watch one video."

These companies aren't evil, necessarily. They're just really good at their job. And their job is to capture your attention and sell it to advertisers. Your focus is the product.

But here's what's happening in your brain while you're scrolling:

Every time you open your phone, your brain releases a small amount of dopamine in anticipation of a reward. This is called the "wanting" phase. Your brain is saying, "Something good might be here!"

Then, when you find something interesting—a funny video, a message from a friend, a post that makes you angry—you get the actual dopamine hit. This is the "liking" phase.

> **Curious fact**
>
> Cues can trigger a stronger dopamine response than the reward itself—anticipation, not enjoyment, drives the next swipe.
>
> (Dialogues in Clinical Neuroscience, 2016)

But here's the trap: the anticipation (wanting) often produces more dopamine than the reward itself (liking). That's why you keep scrolling even when nothing is actually making you happy. Your brain is chasing the anticipation, not the satisfaction.

Neuroscientist Dr. Anna Lembke from Stanford calls this the "pleasure-pain balance." Every time you experience pleasure, your brain automatically tips toward pain to maintain balance. The more intense the pleasure, the deeper the pain that follows.

Think about it like a seesaw. When you get a dopamine spike from your phone, the pleasure side goes up. But immediately, your brain starts pushing the pain side up to restore balance. If you keep triggering pleasure spikes all day long, your baseline shifts. Now you need stimulation just to feel normal.

This is why you feel anxious when you can't check your phone. It's not because something important is happening. It's because your brain is experiencing withdrawal from the constant dopamine drip it's become dependent on.

I discovered this science after months of frustration. I'd tried everything to fix my focus problems—better sleep, more coffee, standing desks, noise-canceling headphones. Nothing worked because I was treating symptoms, not the cause.

The cause was simple: my reward system had been reprogrammed by algorithms designed to be more addictive than slot machines.

And if you're reading this, chances are yours has too.

How Your Brain Became a Pleasure Junkie

Let me share a story that might sound familiar.

Two years ago, I decided to "read more." I bought twelve books that everyone said would change my life. Business books, philosophy, self-help—the works. I was genuinely excited.

I sat down with the first book, determined to finally be one of those people who reads for pleasure. I made it through three pages before my mind wandered. I checked my phone. Replied to a text. Looked at Instagram for "just a second."

Thirty minutes later, I was still on my phone. The book sat closed on the table.

I felt terrible about myself. What was wrong with me? Reading used to be easy. As a kid, I could lose myself in books for hours. Now I couldn't focus for three pages?

Here's what I didn't understand then: I was comparing activities with wildly different dopamine profiles.

Reading a book releases dopamine slowly and steadily. It's like a gentle stream. The reward comes from following the narrative, connecting ideas, and learning something new. It's satisfying, but it's subtle.

Your phone, on the other hand, is like a fire hose of dopamine. Every swipe brings something new. Every notification promises a reward. Your brain gets hit after hit after hit, at a pace that would be impossible in any natural setting.

Now imagine you've been drinking from that fire hose all day, every day, for years. Then someone hands you a gentle stream and says, "Isn't this refreshing?"

> **Quick insight**
> After chronic overstimulation, the brain can cut dopamine receptors by up to 20%—a built-in safety brake that dulls pleasure from normal activities. (Nature Neuroscience, 2015)

It's not that the stream isn't good. It's that your brain has been recalibrated to expect the fire hose. Anything less feels insufficient.

This recalibration happens gradually, which makes it insidious. You don't wake up one day unable to focus. It's more like slowly losing your hearing—you don't notice until someone points out you've been asking them to repeat themselves.

Scientists call this "dopamine downregulation." When your brain gets too much dopamine too often, it reduces the number of dopamine receptors. It's like your brain is turning down the volume to protect itself from being overwhelmed.

But this creates a cruel paradox: now you need more stimulation to feel the same level of reward. Activities that used to bring you joy—reading, conversation, nature walks, creating something—these all become boring because your brain's volume is turned down too low to appreciate them.

I call this becoming a "pleasure junkie" not to be dramatic, but because it's accurate. Like any addict, you need bigger hits to feel normal. And like any addict, you probably don't realize how dependent you've become until you try to stop.

Remember: your brain isn't broken. It's adapted. It did exactly what it's supposed to do when faced with constant overstimulation—it protected itself.

The problem is, in protecting itself from too much pleasure, it destroyed your ability to experience normal amounts of satisfaction.

The Real Cost of Instant Gratification

Let's talk about what this is actually costing you.

I'm not talking about screen time statistics or how many hours you're "wasting." I'm talking about the invisible tax on everything that matters in your life.

The first cost: **your potential**.

Right now, somewhere in your mind, there's a project you've been thinking about for months. Maybe it's a business idea. A creative pursuit. A skill you want to learn. Something that could genuinely change your life.

But every time you sit down to work on it, you can't sustain focus for more than twenty minutes. You get distracted. You check your phone. You open a new tab. And by the end of the day, you've made zero meaningful progress.

This isn't laziness. This is your hijacked dopamine system making hard work feel unrewarding. And every day you don't make progress is another day that idea stays stuck in your head instead of becoming reality.

I lost eighteen months to this. Eighteen months of "working" on projects that never got finished. Eighteen months of starting things with excitement and abandoning them weeks later. Eighteen months of watching less talented people succeed at the exact things I was too scattered to complete.

The second cost: **your relationships**.

When was the last time you had a two-hour conversation with someone you care about, fully present, without checking your phone once?

If you're like most people, you can't remember. Because even when you're not on your phone, part of your mind is still there. You're half-listening while planning what to say next. You're physically present but mentally somewhere else.

People notice this. They may not say anything, but they feel it. They feel the distance. They stop sharing the important stuff because they can sense you're not really there.

I nearly lost relationships I cared about because of this. My girlfriend would be telling me something important, and I'd nod along while my mind calculated the best time to check my Instagram. She eventually stopped sharing things with me. Not because she was angry—because what was the point?

The third cost: **your peace of mind**.

That constant low-level anxiety you feel? That's not normal. That's your brain in a perpetual state of anticipation, always expecting the next notification, the next update, the next hit.

You can't relax anymore. Even when you're doing something enjoyable, there's this background noise in your mind. This restlessness. This feeling that you should be checking something, doing something, consuming something.

True peace—the kind where your mind is quiet and present—becomes impossible. You're always slightly on edge, always slightly unsatisfied, always chasing the next moment instead of experiencing this one.

The fourth cost: **your confidence**.

Every time you tell yourself you'll focus today and then don't, you lose a little bit of trust in yourself. Every project you abandon, every promise you break to yourself, every goal you fail to execute on—it all compounds into a deep, gnawing sense that you're not reliable.

You stop believing in your ability to follow through. And when you don't believe you can do something, you stop trying. Which means your hijacked dopamine system doesn't just steal your attention—it steals your sense of agency in your own life.

> **Research insight**
> Heavy social media use is linked to a 60% higher risk of feeling chronically dissatisfied with personal achievements—a gap driven by constant social comparison and fragmented attention. (American Journal of Preventive Medicine, 2017)

This was the worst part for me. I knew I was capable of more. I had the intelligence, the opportunities, the resources. But I couldn't trust myself to see anything through. And that feeling of watching your potential slip away while being powerless to stop it—that's a special kind of torture.

Here's what nobody tells you about instant gratification: it's not free. Every cheap dopamine hit you get from your phone is paid for with the inability to derive satisfaction from meaningful achievement.

You're trading long-term fulfillment for momentary distraction. And if you keep making that trade, you'll wake up years from now with a perfectly curated Instagram feed and absolutely nothing substantial to show for your life.

The Candy vs Vegetables Effect

Let me give you a metaphor that explains everything.

Imagine you start every morning by eating a bag of candy. Pure sugar, straight into your system. It tastes great. You love it.

Then, for lunch, someone puts a plate of vegetables in front of you. Broccoli, carrots, spinach—healthy stuff.

How does it taste?

Terrible, right? Bland. Boring. Completely unsatisfying compared to the candy.

But here's the question: Are the vegetables actually bad? Or have you just destroyed your taste buds' ability to appreciate them?

Now imagine you fast for twenty-four hours. No food at all. The next day, someone offers you an apple. Not candy—just a regular apple.

Suddenly, that apple tastes incredible. Sweet, crisp, satisfying. Because your taste receptors have reset. You can appreciate normal levels of flavor again. This is exactly what's happening in your brain with dopamine.

> **Neuroscience fact**
> In lab studies, participants who avoided high-sugar foods for just two weeks showed stronger activation in the brain's reward centers when later tasting simple, healthy foods—proof that reward sensitivity can recover quickly. (American Journal of Clinical Nutrition, 2018)

Your phone is the candy. Notifications, social media, endless content—these are pure dopamine sugar. They taste great in the moment, but they're destroying your brain's ability to find reward in normal activities.

Real work—the vegetables—can't compete. Reading, deep conversation, creative projects, exercise, nature—these all release dopamine, but at levels your overstimulated brain barely registers anymore.

So you keep reaching for more candy. More scrolling. More distraction. More instant gratification. Because nothing else feels rewarding enough.

But here's what changes everything: if you remove the candy for long enough, your taste comes back. The vegetables start tasting good again. Actually, they start tasting better than candy ever did, because they provide real nourishment instead of empty calories.

This isn't a metaphor I made up to sound clever. This is literally how your dopamine system works.

When I finally understood this, everything clicked. I wasn't weak. I wasn't lazy. I wasn't fundamentally broken. I had just been eating dopamine candy for so long that I'd forgotten what real satisfaction tasted like.

The same is true for you.

Right now, your brain is telling you that scrolling feels better than working. That checking notifications is more rewarding than having a real conversation. That consuming content is more satisfying than creating something.

But your brain is lying. It's not giving you accurate information about what's actually rewarding. It's giving you information based on a reward system that's been completely distorted by overstimulation.

The good news? Taste can be retrained. Receptors can recover. Your brain can remember what real satisfaction feels like.

But first, you have to stop eating the candy.

And that's what the rest of this book is about: how to reset your dopamine baseline so that meaningful activities feel rewarding again. How to retrain your brain to crave substance instead of stimulation. How to feel naturally motivated instead of constantly forcing yourself to focus.

Your brain isn't broken. It's just been fed the wrong diet for too long.

It's time to change the menu.

Chapter 2:
Diagnosing Your Addiction

"We cannot solve our problems with the same thinking we used when we created them." Albert Einstein

You know something is wrong. You've felt it for months, maybe years. Your attention scatters. Your focus fragments. You can't finish what you start or stay present in conversations. You reach for your phone compulsively, often without conscious decision.

But knowing something is wrong isn't the same as diagnosing what's wrong.

This chapter moves you from vague awareness to specific diagnosis. From "I think I have a problem" to "Here's exactly what the problem is and how severe it's become."

Diagnosis matters because treatment depends on accurate assessment. You can't fix what you haven't properly identified. And you can't measure progress without baseline data.

> **Reflection prompt**
> Before you try to fix your focus, write down three concrete ways distraction shows up in your day. Naming the pattern turns frustration into data—and data is the first step to regaining control.

Most people skip this step. They feel bad about their phone usage or scattered attention, so they try random solutions. Delete an app. Set a timer. Promise themselves they'll "do better." These attempts fail because they're not addressing a measured problem. They're reacting to discomfort without understanding its source.

This chapter gives you the tools to diagnose your actual condition. Not through self-judgment or shame. Through objective measurement and honest assessment.

By the end, you'll know exactly where you stand. How dysregulated your system is. Which specific behaviors are causing the most damage. What your personal triggers are. How your addiction manifests.

That clarity is the foundation for everything that follows.

Quick Self-Check: Early Warning Signs

Before diving into comprehensive assessment, start with a simple question: does your attention system show signs of dysregulation?

Here are eight early warning indicators. If you experience three or more regularly, your dopamine system likely needs attention:

- *You can't maintain focus for more than 20 minutes without feeling the urge to check something.*
- *You feel exhausted even after adequate sleep, yet energized when engaging with high-stimulation content.*
- *Activities that used to bring satisfaction (reading, hobbies, conversations) now feel boring or pointless.*
- *You know what you should be doing but can't make yourself do*

it, despite no external obstacles.
- *You reach for your phone automatically during any pause or moment of waiting.*
- *You consume content (scrolling, watching, reading) without remembering or enjoying what you consumed.*
- *You feel anxious or uncomfortable when separated from your phone for even short periods.*
- *You start tasks enthusiastically but abandon them when they require sustained effort.*

This isn't a comprehensive diagnostic tool. It's a quick temperature check. If several of these resonate, keep reading. The detailed assessment is next.

The Four Types of Modern Addiction

Not all attention problems look the same. Digital overstimulation manifests in different patterns depending on which high-dopamine activities dominate your life.

Understanding which type (or combination of types) describes your pattern helps you design targeted interventions. Most people have a primary type with secondary tendencies.

Type One: The Infinite Scroller

Primary behavior: Social media, news feeds, content platforms. Anything with infinite scroll that provides constant novelty without natural stopping points.

Trigger pattern: Boredom, waiting, transitions between activities. Any empty moment gets filled with scrolling.

Dopamine mechanism: Intermittent reinforcement. Most content is mediocre, but occasionally you find something interesting. This unpredictable reward schedule is highly addictive. Your brain keeps scrolling hoping for the next hit.

Real-world impact: Inability to tolerate understimulation.

Conversations feel slow. Books feel tedious. Nothing in real life can compete with the novelty rate of a well-engineered feed.

The Infinite Scroller's biggest challenge isn't the time spent scrolling. It's the cognitive fragmentation. Even when you're not scrolling, you're thinking about what you might be missing. Your attention is never fully present.

Type Two: The Binge Watcher

Primary behavior: Streaming video content. Netflix, YouTube, streaming platforms. Hours disappear into passive consumption.

Trigger pattern: End of workday, loneliness, stress, decision fatigue. When you need to "turn off your brain," you turn on a screen.

Dopamine mechanism: Narrative engagement plus autoplay. Stories activate your brain's natural narrative processing, and autoplay removes the friction of choosing to continue. One episode becomes five without conscious decision.

Real-world impact: Passive mode becomes default. You lose the capacity for active engagement. Creating anything feels impossible because you're trained to consume. Your brain expects to be entertained rather than to engage.

The Binge Watcher's challenge is distinguishing rest from escape. You think you're relaxing, but hours of passive consumption leave you more depleted than you started. Real rest requires presence. Binge watching is absence.

Type Three: The Digital Achiever

Primary behavior: Productivity apps, email, work-related content, optimization systems. Constantly checking, updating, organizing, optimizing.

Trigger pattern: Any moment of uncertainty or completion. Finished one task, immediately check for the next. Unsure what to do next, check email for direction.

Dopamine mechanism: Completion dopamine and external validation. Each email answered, each task checked off, each notification cleared provides a micro-hit of accomplishment. The feeling is productive, but the actual output is minimal.

Real-world impact: Busy but not productive. Constant activity that doesn't move important projects forward. You're always working but never making significant progress because you're optimizing inputs instead of focusing on meaningful output.

The Digital Achiever's challenge is recognizing that productivity theater isn't productivity. Responding to 50 emails isn't necessarily more valuable than writing one important document. But it feels more immediately rewarding.

Type Four: The Stimulation Stacker

Primary behavior: Multiple stimulation sources simultaneously. Watching shows while scrolling. Listening to podcasts during every activity. Music, videos, and content layered constantly.

Trigger pattern: Any activity that doesn't provide sufficient stimulation alone. Walking, cleaning, commuting, eating. Every activity gets enhanced with additional input.

Dopamine mechanism: Stimulation tolerance. Your baseline for "enough" stimulation has risen so high that normal activities feel insufficient. You need multiple streams of input to feel engaged.

Real-world impact: Complete inability to be present with single activities or your own thoughts. Silence feels intolerable. Being alone with your mind creates anxiety. You've lost access to reflection, processing, and integration because you never give your brain space for those functions.

The Stimulation Stacker's challenge is the most severe. You've trained your brain that baseline reality isn't enough. This makes almost every real-world activity feel inadequate, which drives even more stimulation seeking.

Most people show tendencies across multiple types. You might be primarily an Infinite Scroller with secondary Binge Watcher tendencies. Or a Digital Achiever who also Stimulation Stacks.

> **Did you know?**
> When researchers tracked phone and media multitasking, they found heavy multitaskers scored 11% lower on working-memory tasks and were slower to recover focus after interruptions. (Proceedings of the National Academy of Sciences, 2009)

Identifying your primary pattern helps you understand your specific vulnerabilities and design your reset accordingly. Different types require different intervention strategies.

Your Personal Stimulation Audit

General patterns are useful. Personal data is essential. This section walks you through four assessment exercises that reveal your specific relationship with high-stimulation activities.

Do all four. The combined data gives you a complete picture of your current state.

Exercise One: 48-Hour Tracking

For two consecutive days, track every instance of high-stimulation activity. Not your total screen time. Individual instances of engagement.

Create a simple tally sheet. Every time you pick up your phone, open social media, start watching content, or engage in any high-dopamine activity, make a mark.

Don't change your behavior. Don't try to improve. Just track honestly. You're gathering baseline data, not judging yourself.

At the end of 48 hours, count the marks. The number reveals your engagement frequency. Most people dramatically underestimate how often they're seeking stimulation. They think it's 10-15 times per day. The actual number is usually 50-100+.

This frequency number is your baseline. You'll track it again during and after your reset to measure progress.

Exercise Two: Energy Mapping

For one day, rate your energy level every hour on a scale of 1-10. But also note what you were doing in the hour before each rating.

You're looking for patterns. Which activities energize you? Which deplete you? Which ones you think should be restorative but actually aren't?

Pay special attention to activities you consider "relaxation" or "rest." If you rate them as restorative but your energy is consistently lower after them, that's valuable information. Many high-stimulation activities masquerade as rest but actually drain you.

Real rest increases energy. Fake rest (passive consumption, mindless scrolling) depletes it while feeling temporarily comfortable.

Exercise Three: Replacement Audit

List the high-stimulation activities you engage with most frequently. For each one, ask: "What need is this meeting? What would I do instead if this wasn't available?"

Be specific. "I scroll Instagram" meets what need? Connection? Entertainment? Avoiding discomfort? Seeking validation? All of the above?

And what would you actually do in those moments if Instagram wasn't an option? Not what you wish you would do. What you would realistically do given your current state.

This audit reveals two critical things. First, what genuine needs your high-stimulation activities are (inadequately) meeting. Second, whether you have viable alternatives ready or if elimination will leave a vacuum.

Vacuums get filled with whatever's easiest. If you don't have planned alternatives, you'll default back to old patterns even when you're trying to change.

Exercise Four: Honest Inventory

This is the hardest exercise because it requires complete honesty with yourself. Answer these questions in writing. Don't filter. Don't make yourself look better. Nobody sees this but you.

How much time do you actually spend on high-stimulation activities per day? (Be honest. Track if you're not sure.)

How does that compare to how much time you want to spend on them?

What activities have you stopped doing or do less of because high-stimulation activities have replaced them?

What relationships have weakened because you're less present?

What projects have you not started or completed because your attention is too fragmented?

How do you feel about yourself when you're engaging in high-stimulation activities for extended periods?

How do you feel about yourself when you successfully resist them and do something else?

What would change in your life if you could reclaim full control of your attention?

Your answers reveal where the real costs are. Not the surface-level "I waste time on my phone." The deeper costs to relationships, projects, identity, and self-respect.

These costs matter. They're what will motivate you through the difficult parts of your reset when the initial enthusiasm fades.

When Fun Becomes Dysfunction

There's a line between enjoying high-stimulation activities and being controlled by them. This section helps you determine which side of that line you're on.

The distinction isn't about time spent. Someone can spend three hours on social media as a conscious choice and be fine. Someone else spends thirty minutes compulsively and has a problem.

The difference is control. Can you choose when to engage and when to stop? Or does the activity choose for you?

Use versus compulsion: The key distinctions

You're using an activity (healthy relationship):

- You decide when to start based on conscious choice, not automatic impulse
- You can stop when you intended to stop
- The activity enhances your life without displacing important things
- You feel satisfied rather than depleted after engaging
- You can go days without it and feel fine

You're being used by an activity (problematic relationship):

- You engage automatically without conscious decision
- You continue longer than you intended repeatedly
- The activity displaces sleep, work, relationships, or health
- You feel worse about yourself after engaging but do it anyway

- Going without it creates anxiety, restlessness, or strong discomfort

Most people know which category they're in. They just don't want to admit it because admission requires action.

The phone-in-another-room test

Here's a simple diagnostic: Put your phone in a different room for three hours while you're home and awake. Not at work where you're busy. At home during free time when you could use it.

Then observe yourself. What happens?

If you forget the phone exists and only remember it when the three hours are up, you probably have a healthy relationship with it.

If you think about it frequently but don't feel compelled to get it, you're on the border. Mild dependency, manageable with awareness.

If you feel anxious, restless, or incomplete without it, or if you retrieve it before the three hours are up despite nothing urgent happening, you have a problematic dependency.

> **Try this**
> Put your phone in another room and start a timer. Most people last under 10 minutes before grabbing it again—usually without noticing. (University of Michigan, 2020)

This test works because it isolates the relationship variable. Nothing external forces you to use your phone. You're safe at home. No one needs you urgently. Any pull you feel is pure dependency, not legitimate need.

Most people fail this test. They can't make it three hours without checking their phone even when nothing requires checking. That failure is diagnostic data, not moral failure. It tells you something important about your current state.

The substitution pattern

Another indicator: what happens when you try to stop one high-stimulation activity?

If you successfully stop scrolling social media but immediately increase time spent watching videos, or gaming, or news consumption, you haven't addressed the underlying problem. You've just substituted one source of artificial dopamine for another.

This substitution pattern indicates that your issue isn't with a specific app or activity. It's with your dopamine regulation. Any high-stimulation source will do. You're seeking the neurochemical state, not the specific content.

That's important diagnostic information because it means app-specific solutions won't work. Deleting Instagram won't help if you just spend that time on YouTube instead. You need systemic reset, not activity whack-a-mole.

The Seven Symptoms Checklist

This is your comprehensive diagnostic tool. Seven symptoms that indicate dopamine dysregulation. Each symptom includes recognition criteria and severity assessment.

Rate yourself honestly on each symptom: None (0 points), Mild (1 point), Moderate (2 points), or Severe (3 points). Your total score indicates overall dysregulation level.

Symptom One: The Twenty-Minute Wall

You sit down to focus on something important. A work project, reading, creative work. Within twenty minutes, often less, you feel a strong urge to check something else. Your phone, email, social media. The urge isn't related to the task difficulty. Easy tasks trigger it. Interesting tasks trigger it. You just can't maintain focus without seeking stimulation.

None: You can focus for 60+ minutes regularly without urges to check other things.

Mild: You notice urges around 30-45 minutes but can push through them.

Moderate: You consistently hit urges around 20 minutes and often give in.

Severe: You can't focus for more than 10-15 minutes before you're checking something else.

Symptom Two: Anhedonia (The Pleasure Gap)

Activities that used to bring you satisfaction now feel flat or boring. Reading isn't engaging anymore. Hobbies feel pointless. Conversations seem slow. Nothing in real life provides the same level of interest or excitement it once did. You're not depressed exactly. Things just don't feel rewarding unless they're high-stimulation.

None: You enjoy activities at similar levels to how you always have.

Mild: Some activities feel less satisfying but you can still engage with them.

Moderate: Most low-stimulation activities feel boring; you avoid them when possible.

Severe: Almost nothing feels rewarding except high-stimulation activities; you've stopped most hobbies and interests.

Symptom Three: The Exhaustion Paradox

You're constantly tired despite adequate sleep. Seven, eight hours of rest and you wake up depleted. But when you engage with high-stimulation content (scrolling, watching, gaming), you suddenly have energy. You can stay up hours past when you "should" sleep if you're consuming content. The tiredness isn't physical. It's motivational. You have energy for stimulation but not for normal life.

None: Your energy levels correspond to actual rest and activity patterns.

Mild: You notice slight energy differences between stimulating and non-stimulating activities.

Moderate: Clear energy disparity; you're often tired for normal activities but energized for high-stimulation ones.

Severe: You can barely function for daily tasks but can consume content for hours; sleep schedule is severely disrupted.

Symptom Four: The Knowledge-Action Gap

You know exactly what you should be doing. You know it would benefit you. There are no external obstacles preventing you. But you can't make yourself do it. You sit down to start, then immediately find yourself doing something else. Or you think about starting but never actually begin. The gap between knowing and doing has become a chasm. It's not laziness. It's an inability to initiate and sustain action on things that don't provide immediate stimulation.

None: You generally do what you plan to do without significant internal resistance.

Mild: You notice some procrastination but can usually overcome it within a reasonable timeframe.

Moderate: Significant delay between intention and action; you frequently fail to start things you've planned.

Severe: The gap is so large you've mostly stopped planning; you only do what feels immediately compelling.

Symptom Five: Compulsive Checking

You reach for your phone without deciding to. Your hand moves automatically during any pause. Waiting in line. Sitting at a red light. Between tasks. Waking up. Before bed. The checking isn't in response to a notification. It's automatic. You often unlock your phone, stare at the screen, realize there's nothing to check, and lock it again. Seconds later, you're reaching for it again.

None: You check your phone deliberately when you have specific reasons.

Mild: You notice occasional automatic checking but it's infrequent.

Moderate: You check automatically multiple times per hour; often without specific purpose.

Severe: Nearly constant checking; your phone is in your hand most of your waking hours.

Symptom Six: Memory Gaps

You consume content for hours but can't remember what you consumed. You scroll through hundreds of posts but couldn't summarize three of them. You watch multiple videos but can't recall their content an hour later. You read articles but retain nothing. Your consumption is so passive and fragmented that your brain isn't encoding any of it. You're experiencing content without actually processing it.

None: You remember most of what you consume and can discuss it meaningfully.

Mild: Some content is forgotten but you generally retain main points.

Moderate: You forget most content shortly after consuming it.

Severe: You can't remember what you just consumed minutes ago; consumption is purely automatic.

Symptom Seven: Separation Anxiety

Being without your phone or being unable to access high-stimulation activities creates genuine anxiety. Not mild discomfort. Anxiety. Your heart rate increases. You feel restless or irritable. You can't focus on anything else because you're thinking about what you're missing. Even knowing intellectually that nothing urgent is happening doesn't reduce the feeling. The anxiety is disproportionate to any real risk or consequence.

None: You feel neutral or mildly inconvenienced when separated from your phone.

Mild: You notice you think about your phone but it doesn't significantly affect your mood or function.

Moderate: Clear discomfort when separated; you feel notably relieved when you can access it again.

Severe: Genuine anxiety and inability to function normally without access; you avoid situations where you'd be without your phone.

Your Total Score:

0-4 points: Minimal dysregulation. You may have some habits to optimize but your dopamine system is largely functional.

5-9 points: Mild dysregulation. Your attention is affected but not severely impaired. Targeted interventions and boundary improvements can restore function.

10-14 points: Moderate dysregulation. Significant impact on focus, satisfaction, and daily functioning. You need a structured reset to recover baseline function.

15-21 points: Severe dysregulation. Your dopamine system is heavily impaired. Daily life is significantly compromised. A full 30-day reset is essential, and you may need multiple resets over time.

Your score isn't a judgment. It's data. Higher scores mean you have further to recover, but recovery is still entirely possible. Some of the strongest post-reset outcomes come from people who scored highest because they had the most ground to gain.

Write down your score. You'll reassess using this same checklist after your reset. The comparison will show you exactly how much function you've recovered.

Chapter 3:
The Myth of Willpower

"You can't solve a problem on the same level that it was created. You have to rise above it to the next level."
Albert Einstein

I tried everything. Productivity systems. Habit trackers. Waking at 5 AM. Cold showers. Accountability groups. Digital detoxes that lasted three days. I read books, listened to podcasts, hired coaches. I believed that if I just found the right system or built enough discipline, I could force myself to change.

Nothing worked. Or it would work briefly, then collapse. I'd maintain intense focus for a week, maybe two, then inevitably slide back to scattered attention and compulsive checking. Each failure reinforced the belief that something was fundamentally wrong with me. I wasn't disciplined enough. Didn't want it badly enough. Lacked the character necessary for sustained change.

That belief was wrong. The problem wasn't my character. It was my approach. I was trying to solve a chemistry problem with willpower. That's like trying to fix a car engine with a screwdriver when what you need is a wrench. The tool doesn't work because it's not designed for the problem.

This chapter dismantles the myth that behavior change is primarily about willpower and self-discipline. It's not. Willpower is useful, but it's a limited resource that depletes quickly. Building your entire change strategy on willpower guarantees eventual failure.

What actually works is understanding that you're not fighting a character flaw. You're managing a biological system that's been dysregulated. And biological systems respond to environmental design, not moral effort.

Why You Keep Failing to Change

Here's the pattern you know well: You decide to change. You're motivated. You implement new behaviors. For a few days, maybe a week, you succeed. You feel good about yourself. You think this time is different.

Then something happens. A stressful day. A disrupted routine. A moment of weakness. You break your new pattern once. Then again. Within days, you're back to exactly where you started, wondering what's wrong with you.

Nothing is wrong with you. You're using the wrong tool for the job.

Think about it this way: If you need to hammer a nail into wood, you use a hammer. If you use a screwdriver instead, the nail won't go in. Not because you're weak or incompetent. Because a screwdriver isn't designed to drive nails.

Willpower is a screwdriver. Behavior change rooted in biology requires a hammer. You keep failing not because you lack willpower but because willpower is insufficient for the problem you're solving.

Willpower works for decisions. Should I eat this cookie or not? Should I go to the gym today or skip it? These are single-instance choices where willpower can carry you through.

But attention dysregulation isn't a single-instance choice. It's hundreds of micro-decisions per day, every day, indefinitely. Each time you feel the urge to check your phone. Each time your focus wavers. Each time you're tempted to open a distracting app. Willpower can handle a few of these. Not hundreds daily for weeks or months.

The math doesn't work. You have limited willpower. Attention dysregulation creates unlimited opportunities for willpower depletion. Even if you win 90% of those battles through pure discipline, the 10% you lose will be enough to maintain the dysfunction.

This is why willpower-based approaches fail. Not because you didn't try hard enough. Because the approach is fundamentally mismatched to the problem.

Environment Beats Motivation Every Time

If willpower isn't the answer, what is? Environment design.

Your environment shapes behavior more powerfully than your intentions do. Not sometimes. Always. The path of least resistance determines what you actually do, regardless of what you want to do.

If your phone sits on your desk within arm's reach, you'll check it constantly. Not because you're weak. Because it's there, and checking it is effortless. The friction between impulse and action is zero.

If that same phone is in another room, you'll check it far less. Not because your willpower increased. Because the friction increased. You have to stand up, walk to the other room, retrieve the phone, and walk back. That friction gives you space to notice the impulse and choose whether to act on it.

Same person. Same phone. Same temptation. Different environment. Completely different behavior.

This is the core principle of environment design: make good behaviors easy and bad behaviors hard. Structure your physical and digital space so that the actions you want to take require minimal friction while actions you want to avoid require significant friction.

Here's what this looks like practically:

Physical environment design:

Remove high-stimulation devices from your primary living and working spaces. Your phone doesn't belong on your desk, nightstand, or dining table. It belongs in a drawer, another room, or a specific charging location that requires deliberate retrieval.

Create dedicated spaces for specific activities. One space for work. Another for rest. Another for eating. Don't let activities bleed together. When every space is multi-purpose, every space triggers every behavior. Separation creates mental clarity about what you do where.

Eliminate visual triggers. If seeing your gaming console makes you want to play, put it in a closet. If seeing your TV makes you want to watch, cover it or remove it from your bedroom. Out of sight isn't just out of mind. It's out of impulse range.

Digital environment design:

Delete apps from your phone that you compulsively check. Not logged out. Deleted. The friction of reinstalling is usually enough to interrupt the automatic checking pattern.

Use website blockers on your computer. Freedom, Cold Turkey, or browser extensions that block specific sites during specific hours. Make accessing distracting sites require deliberate override, not just a thoughtless click.

Turn off all non-essential notifications. Social media notifications. News alerts. Email badges. Anything that pulls your attention without your permission. Your attention should be pull-based (you decide when to check), not push-based (apps decide when to interrupt you).

Temporal environment design:

Schedule your day in blocks. Deep work blocks with zero distractions. Shallow work blocks for email and administrative tasks. Rest blocks with no screens. Each block has clear boundaries about what's allowed.

Create rituals that mark transitions between modes. A specific sequence of actions that signals to your brain "focus time begins now" or "work is done, rest begins." Rituals reduce the decision fatigue of constantly choosing what to do next.

The power of environment design is that it works without requiring constant willpower. You design once, then the environment does the work of guiding your behavior. Your intentional choices at the design stage replace hundreds of daily willpower decisions.

This doesn't mean you never need willpower. It means you're not depending on willpower to fight hundreds of daily battles. You've removed most of the battles by making unwanted behaviors harder to execute.

The Depletion Trap

Even when you understand that willpower is limited, you might not realize just how quickly it depletes. Or how that depletion creates a vicious cycle that makes behavior change nearly impossible.

Roy Baumeister's research on ego depletion demonstrated that willpower functions like a muscle. Use it intensely and it gets tired. Unlike physical muscles that recover with rest, willpower depletes throughout the day and only fully replenishes with sleep.

Every decision you make consumes willpower. Not just big decisions. Every decision. What to wear. What to eat. Which task to do first. Whether to respond to that message now or later. By afternoon, you've made hundreds of micro-decisions. Your willpower reserves are depleted.

This is why most people break their diets in the evening. Why you can maintain focus all morning but scroll mindlessly after dinner. Why you succeed at avoiding your phone during work but can't stop checking it at night. Not because you suddenly lost discipline. Because your willpower is exhausted.

Kathleen Vohs's research on decision fatigue showed that even trivial choices deplete willpower. People who made a series of inconsequential decisions (choosing between similar products) showed reduced self-control on subsequent unrelated tasks. The decisions didn't need to be important to cause depletion. They just needed to require choice.

Now consider a typical day trying to resist digital distraction through willpower alone:

Morning: You wake up and immediately feel the urge to check your phone. You resist. Willpower used.

Breakfast: You want to scroll while eating. You resist. More willpower used.

Commute: You want to listen to a podcast. You resist to give your mind rest. More willpower used.

Work: Every five minutes, you feel the urge to check email or social media. Each resistance uses willpower. By 10 AM, you've resisted 30 times. Significant willpower depletion.

This continues all day. Hundreds of resistance moments. Each one draining your finite willpower reserves. By evening, you have nothing left. You break. You scroll for two hours, watch content, check everything compulsively.

Then you feel terrible about breaking, which triggers the next morning's determination to do better. The cycle repeats.

This is the depletion trap. Willpower-based resistance creates its own failure through exhaustion. The more you try to white-knuckle through urges, the faster you deplete willpower, the more inevitable failure becomes.

The trap has another insidious element: the resistance itself becomes associated with the behavior you're resisting. Each time you resist checking your phone, you're thinking about checking your phone. The act of resistance keeps the behavior mentally active, actually strengthening the neural pathways you're trying to weaken.

This is why "don't think about pink elephants" makes you think about pink elephants. The instruction not to do something requires holding that thing in mind. Constant resistance to phone checking means constant mental activation of phone checking.

The solution isn't stronger willpower. The solution is reducing the number of times you need to use willpower. That's where environment design becomes essential. When your phone isn't accessible, you don't need willpower to resist checking it. The resistance opportunity never arises. No willpower consumed. No depletion. No trap.

Building Systems Instead of Resolutions

Resolutions are declarations of intent. Systems are structures that make specific outcomes likely. Resolutions depend on motivation and willpower. Systems depend on design and environment.

"I will check my phone less" is a resolution. It fails because it provides no structure for how to actually check your phone less when the urge arises.

A system approach: "My phone lives in a drawer in another room during work hours. I check it twice daily at scheduled times: noon and 6 PM." This provides structure. The behavior happens automatically once the system is in place.

Here's how to build systems that actually work:

The Friction Hierarchy

Not all behaviors need the same level of difficulty. Some should be eliminated entirely. Others should be reduced. Others should be maintained but controlled.

Create three categories:

Eliminated: High-stimulation activities that provide no real value and cause significant harm. These need maximum friction. Delete apps entirely. Block websites permanently. Make access so difficult that it's effectively impossible.

Reduced: Activities that have some value but you're currently overusing. These need moderate friction. Keep the apps but move them off your home screen into folders. Set time limits. Schedule specific usage windows.

Maintained: Activities that are genuinely valuable and not problematic. These need minimal friction. Keep them easily accessible.

Most people don't differentiate. They try to reduce everything through willpower. That's too many battles. The Friction Hierarchy lets you fight fewer, more important battles while accepting controlled use of less problematic activities.

The Replacement Protocol

Never eliminate a behavior without planning what replaces it. Empty space gets filled with whatever's easiest, which is usually the behavior you just eliminated.

For each high-friction activity, identify:

What need was it meeting? (Entertainment, connection, avoiding discomfort, filling time)

What healthier activity could meet that need? (Not what should meet it. What actually could.)

What preparation makes the replacement accessible when the urge hits?

Example: You eliminate evening scrolling. What need was that meeting? Probably decompression after work and avoiding the discomfort of being alone with your thoughts.

Replacement: Reading physical books for 30 minutes. This provides mental decompression while training sustained attention.

Preparation: Have books ready on your couch where you used to scroll. Make the replacement easier than finding your phone.

Schedule-Based Boundaries

Willpower-based boundaries ("I won't check my phone too much") are vague and exhausting. Schedule-based boundaries ("I check my phone at 9 AM, noon, 3 PM, and 6 PM for 10 minutes each") are clear and automatic.

Time-based rules require one decision (creating the schedule) instead of continuous decisions (whether to check now). Once the schedule exists, you're not deciding whether to check. You're following the schedule. This dramatically reduces willpower consumption.

The schedule must be realistic. Don't create aspirational schedules you can't maintain. Start with a schedule that feels almost too easy, then tighten it gradually as adherence becomes automatic.

Accountability Structures

External accountability makes following systems easier because it adds social cost to breaking them. You're not just letting yourself down. You're letting someone else down.

Find one person who understands your goals and check in with them weekly. Not to report success. To report both successes and failures honestly. The expectation of reporting creates helpful pressure to maintain your systems.

Alternatively, financial commitment works. Give someone $500 with instructions to donate it to a cause you'd hate to support if you don't maintain your systems for 30 days. The financial stake makes casual abandonment much harder.

Progressive Challenge

Don't implement all systems simultaneously. Start with the system that will have the biggest impact with the least disruption. Master that before adding another.

This progressive approach prevents overwhelm and builds confidence. Each successful system gives you proof that systems work, which makes implementing the next one easier.

Week one: Phone stays in another room during work hours. Week two: Add evening wind-down routine with no screens one hour before bed. Week three: Add scheduled checking times instead of constant availability. Week four: Add replacement activities for eliminated behaviors.

By week four, you have four systems working automatically instead of one overwhelming system you couldn't maintain.

Brain Chemistry vs Character Flaws

Here's what you need to understand at the deepest level: your attention problems aren't moral failures. They're biological states.

When your dopamine receptors are downregulated from chronic overstimulation, you experience real, physical difficulty focusing on normal-reward activities. This isn't "being lazy." This is neurochemistry. Your brain literally registers normal activities as less rewarding than they should be.

When you compulsively check your phone, you're not weak. You're experiencing a conditioned response that's been reinforced thousands of times. Your brain has learned a pattern: discomfort → phone checking → temporary relief. That's operant conditioning, not character flaw.

When you know you should do something important but can't make yourself start, you're not lazy. You're experiencing a mismatch between your goal-oriented prefrontal cortex and your reward-prediction system. Your executive function wants to work. Your dopamine system isn't providing the motivational fuel to initiate. That's a chemical problem, not a willpower problem.

This reframe isn't about removing responsibility. You're still responsible for addressing the problem. But you address it through the right mechanisms: resetting your brain chemistry and redesigning your environment. Not through moral self-flagellation and willpower battles.

The shame and guilt you feel about your attention problems aren't helping you change. They're making change harder. Shame triggers stress responses that further dysregulate your system. Guilt consumes mental energy you need for implementing solutions.

You don't need more shame. You need accurate diagnosis and effective intervention.

Think of it this way: If you had diabetes, you wouldn't try to lower your blood sugar through willpower and self-criticism. You'd adjust your diet, take medication if needed, and monitor your glucose levels. Same principle applies here. Your dopamine system is dysregulated. You need to adjust your inputs, implement interventions, and monitor your progress.

Nobody tells diabetics they just need more discipline to normalize their insulin response. Nobody should tell you that you just need more discipline to normalize your dopamine response.

The path forward isn't about becoming a better person. You're not a bad person who needs fixing. You're a person with a specific, treatable problem who needs the right intervention. That intervention starts with stopping the behaviors that maintain dysregulation and building the structures that support regulation. Not through heroic daily willpower battles. Through systematic environmental design and neurochemical reset. You're not fighting a character flaw. You're managing a biological system. Treat it accordingly.

Chapter 4:
Preparing For The Reset

"By failing to prepare, you are preparing to fail." Benjamin Franklin

A dopamine reset isn't something you just decide to do and wing it. It's a structured intervention that requires specific preparation. Skip the preparation, and you're not just reducing your chances of success. You're guaranteeing failure.

Think of it like surgery. You wouldn't let a doctor operate on you without sterilizing the tools, mapping the procedure, and having a recovery plan ready. The same principle applies here.

This chapter is about the work that happens before the work. The setup that makes everything else possible. The decisions you make now that determine whether your reset succeeds or becomes another abandoned attempt.

If you're tempted to skip this chapter and jump straight to the protocol, don't. The time you invest in preparation will save you weeks of false starts and frustration.

Setting Your Baseline and Goals

You can't measure progress without knowing where you started. And you can't know if you've arrived without defining where you're going.

You already gathered some preliminary data during your earlier audit. Now we'll formalize those numbers as your official baseline and add crucial subjective measurements.

Finalizing Your Baseline Metrics

Pull together the tracking data you collected earlier and add these new measurements:

Rate your mental clarity on a scale of one to ten. Be honest. If your mind feels foggy most of the time, that's important data. Track this at three points each day for three days: morning, afternoon, and evening.

> **Pro tip**
> Set goals you can *count*, not just *feel*. If you can't measure it in numbers or checkboxes, it's not a target—it's a wish.

Rate your end-of-day satisfaction. Again, one to ten. Are you proud of what you accomplished, or disappointed? This reveals whether your activity patterns are actually serving your goals.

Measure your decision-making speed. Time how long it takes you to make three simple decisions: what to eat for lunch, which task to do first in your morning, what to wear. Slow decision-making indicates depleted cognitive resources.

Count your genuine accomplishments per week. Not busy work or tasks checked off. Real accomplishments that move meaningful projects forward. This number reveals your true productivity versus activity theater.

Write all of this down in one place. These numbers are your baseline. Everything you do from this point forward will be measured against them.

When I did this exercise, my mental clarity averaged 3.8 out of 10. My end-of-day satisfaction was consistently below 4. Simple decisions were taking me five to ten minutes. I was averaging 1.5 genuine accomplishments per week despite feeling busy constantly.

Seeing it quantified was brutal. But it was also clarifying. I finally had objective data instead of vague dissatisfaction.

Defining Your Targets

Now that you know where you are, decide where you want to go. Be specific.

Don't say "use my phone less." Say "reduce phone unlocks to under

30 per day within four weeks."

Don't say "focus better." Say "work in uninterrupted 90-minute blocks three times per week by the end of month one."

Don't say "feel more productive." Say "complete two major projects that have been sitting unfinished for over a month."

Vague goals produce vague results. Specific goals produce measurable progress.

Here's a framework for setting effective targets:

Choose three primary metrics to improve. Don't try to fix everything at once. Maybe it's mental clarity rating, genuine accomplishments per week, and focus block completion. Or end-of-day satisfaction, decision speed, and project completion rate. Pick the three that matter most to your situation.

Set 30-day targets for each metric. Make them challenging but achievable. If your mental clarity is currently averaging 4, aiming for 10 is unrealistic. Aiming for 7 is reasonable.

Define what success looks like beyond the numbers. How will you feel when you're focusing better? What will you do with your reclaimed time and attention? What projects will you complete? Paint the picture.

Identify potential obstacles specific to your life. What unique situations trigger your phone use? When is your willpower lowest? What excuses have derailed past attempts at change? Write them all down so you can plan for them.

Create milestone checkpoints. Don't just measure at day 30. Check progress at day 7, 14, and 21. This allows you to adjust your approach if something isn't working rather than discovering at the end that the entire month was wasted.

The goal here isn't to create a rigid plan you'll beat yourself up for not following perfectly. The goal is to establish clear enough targets that you can tell whether you're making progress.

Without baselines and targets, you're flying blind. With them, you have instruments that tell you exactly where you are and where you're headed.

Identifying Your Biggest Triggers

Your phone checking isn't random. Your scrolling isn't arbitrary. Your focus breakdowns happen in response to specific triggers that you probably haven't consciously identified.

This section is about mapping those triggers so you can plan defenses before you need them.

Emotional Triggers

The most common triggers are emotional. You reach for stimulation when you feel something uncomfortable.

Boredom is the obvious one. The moment there's nothing demanding your attention, you fill the gap with your phone. But boredom isn't the only trigger.

Anxiety makes people seek distraction. When you're worried about something, scrolling feels like escape. It's not, but your brain thinks it is.

Frustration triggers checking. When a task gets difficult, your brain offers an easier alternative. "This is too hard. Let's see what's happening on social media."

Loneliness drives social media use. When you feel disconnected, you reach for the digital version of connection, even though it usually makes loneliness worse.

Inadequacy sends people scrolling through others' highlight reels. When you doubt yourself, seeing others succeed somehow feels both painful and compulsive.

Track your emotional state right before you reach for your phone. Do this for three days. You'll see patterns emerge.

When I did this tracking, I discovered most of my checking happened during creative work when I hit a difficult section. The frustration of not knowing how to proceed sent me straight to my phone. I wasn't avoiding work. I was avoiding the specific discomfort of being stuck.

Situational Triggers

Certain situations reliably trigger stimulation-seeking behavior.

Waiting in line. Sitting in a waiting room. Commercial breaks. Any moment of enforced idleness. These are high-risk situations because your brain interprets them as opportunities for easy dopamine.

Transitions between tasks. You finish one thing and before starting the next, you check your phone. Not because anything important happened, but because transitions create small gaps that your brain wants to fill.

Meals eaten alone. Without conversation, you default to your phone as a dining companion.

First thing in the morning and last thing at night. These bookend moments are particularly dangerous because they set the dopamine baseline for waking hours and disrupt sleep recovery.

Social situations where you feel uncomfortable. Parties, networking events, anywhere you feel slightly out of place. Your phone becomes a security blanket.

Write down your high-risk situations. Be specific. "Work" isn't specific enough. "After I finish a major task but before I start planning the next one" is specific.

Environmental Triggers

Your physical environment contains cues that trigger automatic behaviors.

Your phone's location is the most obvious. If it's on your desk, you'll check it. If it's in your pocket, you'll check it. If it's visible, you'll check it.

Certain locations have associations. Maybe your couch is where you always scroll. Your bed is where you watch YouTube. Your desk is where you get distracted by tabs.

Sounds trigger checking. Notification sounds, obviously. But also ambient noise that makes you think you heard a notification. Even silence can be a trigger if you're used to background stimulation.

Visual cues matter too. Seeing someone else on their phone makes you want to check yours. Seeing a notification badge. Seeing your charger means your battery is low, which creates urgency to check before it dies.

Objects trigger rituals. Your morning coffee might be associated with scrolling. Your commute bag might trigger podcast listening. Your evening couch time might mean Netflix autoplay.

Map these environmental triggers. Walk through a typical day and note every physical cue that precedes phone checking.

The Trigger Matrix

Once you've identified your triggers, create a simple matrix. Three columns: Trigger, Current Response, Planned Alternative.

For example:

Trigger: Hit a difficult section during creative work Current Response: Check phone to "give brain a break" Planned Alternative: Stand up, walk to window, look outside for two minutes

Trigger: Waiting in line Current Response: Automatically pull out phone Planned Alternative: Practice observing surroundings, notice three things I've never noticed before

Trigger: Transition between tasks Current Response: Check social media Planned Alternative: Close eyes, take five deep breaths, visualize next task

Trigger: Feel inadequate about progress Current Response: Scroll through others' success stories Planned Alternative: Write down one thing I accomplished today, no matter how small

The goal isn't to eliminate triggers. That's impossible. The goal is to have a planned response ready before the trigger happens, so you're not relying on willpower in the moment.

This preparation makes all the difference. When you know frustration during creative work is a trigger and you've already decided you'll look out the window instead of scrolling, the decision is made. You're not fighting temptation. You're executing a plan.

Creating Your Detox Blueprint

This is where we move from analysis to action. You've measured your baseline, set your targets, and identified your triggers. Now you need a concrete plan for the reset itself.

A blueprint isn't a rigid schedule. It's a flexible framework that adapts to your life while maintaining core principles.

There are three levels of dopamine reset, each with different intensity and time requirements.

- The Micro Reset lasts 48 hours. You remove only the highest-dopamine activities while maintaining normal life. This works for people who need to see quick results to stay motivated, or who can't take time away from responsibilities.
- The Standard Reset lasts 7-14 days. This is the sweet spot for most people. Long enough to see significant changes, short enough to be sustainable.
- The Deep Reset lasts 21-30 days. This is for people with severe dopamine dysregulation or those who want complete transformation. It's harder but produces the most dramatic

results.

Which should you choose? Honestly assess your situation.

If your baseline metrics show severe impairment, if you checked most boxes in the seven symptoms list, if past reset attempts failed within days, go for the Standard or Deep Reset.

If you're relatively functional but want optimization, if you have demanding work that can't be paused, start with a Micro Reset and extend if it's going well.

Defining Your Boundaries

For each reset type, define exactly what's in and what's out.

Complete elimination activities: These are totally off-limits during your reset. For most people, this includes social media, news sites, YouTube browsing, and gaming. Be specific about which apps and websites.

Reduced activities: These aren't eliminated but are severely restricted. Maybe you check email twice per day at scheduled times. Maybe you watch one pre-chosen show per week instead of binge-watching.

Permitted activities: These are allowed without restriction. Reading books, physical exercise, face-to-face conversations, creating something, walking without headphones. Make a clear list.

Work necessities: If you need certain digital tools for work, define exactly how you'll use them. Email for work communication but not personal browsing. Slack for team coordination but notifications off except during two designated hours.

The key is removing ambiguity. "I'll use social media less" is ambiguous. "Instagram and Twitter deleted from phone, desktop access blocked except Sundays 4-5 PM" is clear.

Write this down as a contract with yourself. During my first successful reset, I printed mine out and signed it. Sounds dramatic, but it helped me take it seriously.

Designing Your Schedule

Structure your day to support focus, not fight against your natural rhythms.

Morning protocol: Decide exactly what you'll do for the first 90 minutes after waking. No phone, no news, no email. What will you do instead? Exercise, meditation, journaling, reading, making breakfast slowly? Plan it specifically.

Focus blocks: Schedule three 90-minute sessions per week minimum. Mark them in your calendar like important meetings you can't miss. During these blocks, environment is optimized and distractions are eliminated.

Transition rituals: Create specific activities for transitions between tasks. Not checking your phone. Maybe a two-minute breathing exercise, a quick walk, or simply closing your eyes for ten breaths. These rituals signal to your brain that you're shifting gears intentionally, not impulsively.

Evening wind-down: Define when screens stop. One hour before bed minimum. Two hours is better. What will you do instead? Read physical books, talk to family, prepare for tomorrow, stretch?

Weekly review: Schedule one hour per week to review your metrics, adjust your approach, and plan the week ahead. This keeps you honest and allows course correction.

Don't try to optimize every hour of every day. That's exhausting. Create islands of structure in a sea of flexibility.

Preparing Your Environment

You already optimized parts of your environment earlier. Now extend that work systematically to every area of your life where triggers exist.

Focus on new elements you haven't addressed yet:

Create spatial boundaries: Designate your bedroom as a phone-free zone starting one week before your reset. Make your kitchen table a place for meals and conversation only, never for screens. Establish your workspace as sacred ground where only work-related tools exist.

Prepare communication templates: Write short messages you can send to people explaining your reduced availability. "Doing a digital reset for two weeks. Will respond to urgent matters only. Back fully on [date]." Having these ready prevents the excuse of "I need to tell people first."

Set up accountability visibility: If you live with others, tell them your reset schedule and ask them to notice if you're breaking it. Sometimes external observation is enough to interrupt automatic behaviors.

Stock your replacement supplies: Before day one, have everything ready. Books you want to read on your nightstand. Art supplies if you're going to draw. Running shoes by the door if you're going to exercise. Journal and pen on your desk. Remove the friction from good behaviors before you need them.

This isn't just repeating environment design. This is extending it to every corner of your life with specific attention to the unique triggers you've identified.

Building Your Support System

You can do this alone, but you don't have to. And honestly, you probably shouldn't.

The right support system dramatically increases your chances of success. The wrong support system sabotages you. Most people don't think about this ahead of time and end up with neither.

Finding Your Accountability Partner

The ideal accountability partner is someone who understands what you're trying to do, supports the goal, and will be honest with you about your progress.

Not a cheerleader who tells you everything is fine when it's not. Not a critic who makes you feel worse. Someone who can say, "You said you'd focus for three hours today but you only did ninety minutes. What happened?" without judgment but with clarity.

This could be a friend, family member, colleague, or someone from an online community doing the same reset. What matters is that they're invested in your success and willing to check in regularly.

Set up a specific structure. Maybe you text them every evening with your metrics for the day. Maybe you have a weekly call to discuss challenges. Maybe they're the person you call when you're about to break your reset.

Give them permission to be direct. Tell them explicitly that you want honest feedback, not reassurance.

When I did my first serious reset, my accountability partner and I shared daily numbers and created a simple consequence system for missing targets. The structure mattered more than the consequence itself.

Creating a Stimulus-Free Space

You need at least one physical location where no digital temptation exists. A room in your house, a corner of a library, a park bench. Somewhere you can go when you need complete escape from triggers.

For me, it was my kitchen table with my phone in a different room. Nothing fancy. But it became my sanctuary for focus because no associations with distraction existed there.

Set up this space before your reset begins. Test it. Make sure it works. Have everything you need already there so you're not using "I need to get something" as an excuse to go back to the distracting environment.

Building Your Emergency Protocol

You will have moments where the urge to break your reset feels overwhelming. Plan for these moments ahead of time.

Create a list of five things you can do instead of giving in. Make it physical, write it down, keep it accessible. When the urge hits and your willpower is depleted, you don't want to have to think creatively. You want a preset list you can execute.

My emergency protocol:

1. Go for a ten-minute walk outside without my phone
2. Call my accountability partner
3. Do fifty push-ups
4. Take a cold shower
5. Read three pages of a physical book

Yours will be different based on what actually works for your brain and situation. The point is having it ready before you need it.

Test these interventions before your reset. Don't wait until you're in crisis mode to discover that a cold shower doesn't actually help you. Find out what genuinely interrupts the compulsion and put those things on your list.

Joining or Creating a Reset Group

Doing this with others creates momentum and reduces the feeling of isolation. You're not weird or broken. You're part of a group addressing a common problem.

This could be an online community, a group chat with friends, or a local meetup. The format doesn't matter. The shared experience does.

In a group, you can share wins and struggles, get advice from people further along, and provide support to people just starting. The accountability is built in.

When one person shares that they made it three days without checking social media, it inspires everyone else. When someone admits they broke their reset, others can help them analyze what happened and get back on track.

If you can't find a group, create one. Post in a community online. Ask friends if they're interested. You might be surprised how many people are dealing with the same issues and would welcome structure around addressing them.

The Replacement Strategy

This is the section that determines whether your reset succeeds or fails. Pay close attention.

Your brain needs stimulation. Not the unhealthy kind, but some kind. If you remove all sources of dopamine without replacing them, you're not resetting your system. You're just torturing yourself until you crack.

The Replacement Strategy is about installing better sources of dopamine before you remove the bad ones.

Understanding Dopamine Hierarchies

Not all dopamine is created equal. Some sources are quick and empty. Others are slower but more satisfying.

High dopamine, low value: Social media scrolling, news checking, random YouTube videos. These spike your dopamine fast but leave you feeling worse.

Medium dopamine, medium value: Watching a good show, playing a game with friends, having a meandering conversation. These provide enjoyment without destruction.

Lower dopamine, high value: Reading a challenging book, creating something, solving a difficult problem, having a deep conversation. These release dopamine more slowly but build lasting satisfaction.

The goal isn't to eliminate all quick dopamine sources. That's unrealistic. The goal is to shift your baseline so you primarily get dopamine from the high-value sources, with occasional medium-value sources, and minimal low-value sources.

Installing Replacements Before Removal

Two weeks before your reset officially starts, begin introducing replacement activities.

If you're going to remove evening scrolling, start reading physical books in the evening now. Get into the habit before you need to rely on it.

If you're going to stop checking your phone first thing in the morning, start a morning routine now that doesn't include your phone.

If you're going to eliminate podcast listening during all activities, start experiencing silence during walks and commutes now.

This pre-installation period makes the actual reset vastly easier because you're not forming new habits under duress. You're just expanding habits that already exist.

Track how these new activities feel. Some replacements will work better than others. A book that bores you won't replace scrolling successfully. Find the activities that actually engage you enough to compete with digital stimulation.

The Activity Menu

Create a literal menu of replacement activities, categorized by how much time and energy they require.

Five-minute options: Breathing exercises, looking out a window, stretching, making tea, petting your dog, writing three sentences in a journal.

Twenty-minute options: Going for a walk, calling a friend, reading a chapter, journaling properly, organizing one drawer, cooking something simple.

Hour-plus options: Working on a project, cooking a real meal, exercising, having a deep conversation, creating something, learning a skill.

When the urge to check your phone or scroll hits, consult your menu. Pick something that matches your available time and current energy level.

The existence of the menu removes the decision-making burden. You're not trying to think of something to do while your brain is screaming for a dopamine hit. You're just choosing from pre-approved options.

Laminate this menu or put it somewhere visible. Make it a physical object you can reference without needing your phone.

Embracing Boredom as Medicine

Here's the hardest part of the Replacement Strategy: sometimes the replacement is nothing.

Sometimes you need to sit with boredom. Actively practice it. Not because boredom is fun, but because your brain needs to relearn that not being stimulated is okay.

Schedule fifteen minutes per day during your reset where you do absolutely nothing. No phone, no book, no music, no activity. Just sit. Be bored.

This sounds unbearable, and at first it is. Your brain will generate every possible excuse for why this is stupid and you should stop. Push through.

By day seven, those fifteen minutes will feel different. Still not enjoyable, but tolerable. Your brain will have remembered that boredom isn't dangerous. It's just boring.

This recalibration is essential. Without it, you'll always need something filling every moment. With it, you develop the capacity to be present without needing constant input.

Tracking Your Replacements

For the first two weeks of your reset, track which replacement activities you use and how they feel.

After reading for thirty minutes instead of scrolling, rate your satisfaction one to ten. After going for a walk instead of checking your phone, note your energy level and mental clarity.

You'll discover which replacements actually work for you and which don't. The activities that leave you feeling better than before are the ones to prioritize. The ones that feel like punishment are the ones to adjust or replace.

The Replacement Strategy isn't about finding perfect alternatives to phone use. It's about building a portfolio of activities that together provide enough satisfaction that your brain doesn't feel constantly deprived.

With replacements in place, your reset becomes sustainable. Without them, it becomes a countdown to relapse.

Chapter 5:
The 30-day Dopamine detox

"The secret of change is to focus all of your energy not on fighting the old, but on building the new." Socrates

This is it. The protocol itself. Everything up to this point has been preparation. Understanding the problem, measuring your baseline, identifying triggers, building systems. Now you're going to execute.

But here's what you need to understand before we begin: this isn't going to feel good at first. Your brain will resist. Hard. It's been running on artificial dopamine for so long that normal stimulation levels will feel like deprivation.

That discomfort isn't a sign that something is wrong. It's a sign that something is finally being fixed.

> **Reminder**
> Discomfort is data. When withdrawal hits, it's not punishment—it's your brain recalibrating to baseline. Don't chase relief; track the reset.

The 30-day protocol is divided into five distinct phases, each with its own focus and challenges. Some days will be harder than others. Some phases will feel impossible while you're in them and obvious in retrospect.

Your job isn't to enjoy this process. Your job is to complete it.

The payoff comes later. Much later than your dopamine-hijacked brain wants. But it comes. And when it does, you'll understand why every uncomfortable moment was worth it.

Let's begin.

Days 1-2: The Discomfort Phase

The first 48 hours are about one thing: surviving the initial shock to your system.

When you remove the constant dopamine drip your brain has been running on, it reacts like you've taken away oxygen. Panic, restlessness, irritability, and an overwhelming urge to "just check one thing" will dominate these two days.

This is normal. This is expected. This is your brain in withdrawal.

Your primary goal for days one and two is simple: don't break. That's it. Don't worry about being productive. Don't worry about feeling good. Just make it through without giving in to the urge to return to high-stimulation activities.

Here's what will happen hour by hour.

Hour one feels manageable. You're motivated, determined, riding the initial wave of commitment. You'll probably feel good about yourself. This is the easiest hour you'll have for a while.

Hours two through four get progressively harder. Your brain starts sending signals that something is wrong. You'll feel restless. Your hands will want to reach for your phone even though you've removed it from reach.

Hours five through eight are the worst. This is when most people break. The discomfort intensifies. Boredom becomes unbearable. Your brain will invent urgent reasons to check something.

During these hours, execute your prewritten Emergency Protocol from Chapter 4.4 without negotiating. Walk, do push-ups, call your accountability partner. Whatever you planned, execute it. Over and over if necessary.

Hours nine through sixteen level off slightly. The acute panic subsides into dull discomfort. You'll still feel restless, but it's more manageable. This is where you start noticing how often you used stimulation to fill empty moments.

Waiting for water to boil feels interminable. Standing in line becomes torture. Any pause in activity reveals how dependent you've become on constant input.

Sit with this awareness. Don't fix it yet. Just notice it.

Evening of day one is dangerous because you're tired and your willpower is depleted. This is when your evening wind-down routine matters most. Stick to it religiously. No screens an hour before bed. Read physical books. The first night of better sleep starts here.

> **Survival tip**
> Cravings peak fast and fade fast—most last under 15 minutes if you don't feed them. When it hits, start a timer and ride the wave instead of fighting it. (Journal of Behavioral Addictions, 2019)

Day two typically feels worse than day one. The novelty has worn off and the discomfort remains. Your brain has had time to mount a serious counteroffensive. You'll experience stronger urges, more convincing rationalizations, and deeper boredom.

This is the day most people quit. Don't be most people.

On day two, your task is to notice patterns. When are the urges strongest? What emotional states trigger them? Which replacement activities actually help versus which ones feel like punishment?

Write this down. Data collected during discomfort is invaluable for later phases.

By the end of day two, something subtle shifts. The acute withdrawal symptoms start to ease. You've proven to yourself that you can survive without constant stimulation. This proof matters more than you realize. It's the first crack in the belief that you need your phone to function.

Practical strategies for days one and two:

Your elimination activities are completely off-limits. Not reduced. Eliminated. No negotiations. Your brain will try to find loopholes. The boundaries you set are non-negotiable for all 30 days. This is the only time you'll hear this warning because these first 48 hours are when the temptation to negotiate is strongest.

Schedule every hour. Don't leave gaps where boredom can ambush you. Have specific activities planned for every waking hour. This isn't sustainable long-term, but for 48 hours, it keeps you from white-knuckling through empty time.

Increase physical activity. Your body needs to burn the restless energy somehow. Walk more. Exercise more. Move more. Physical exhaustion helps with the mental discomfort.

Tell people you're unavailable. Set up auto-responders. Put up boundaries. You can't focus on resetting if you're worried about disappointing others with slow responses.

Mark each urge on paper. One tally mark per urge. By the end of day two, the number reveals your dependency level.

Sleep as much as you need. Your brain is working hard to recalibrate. If you're tired, sleep. This isn't the time to prove you can function on five hours.

The discomfort of days one and two serves a purpose. It shows you how dependent you've become. It proves the severity of the problem. And it begins the process of teaching your brain that discomfort isn't dangerous.

You're not trying to feel good yet. You're trying to reset the baseline. Discomfort is the price of admission.

Pay it.

Days 3-7: Breaking Point and Breakthrough

Day three is where something interesting happens. The acute

withdrawal eases slightly, but you're not feeling better yet. You're in the gap between the old system breaking down and the new system coming online.

This gap is uncomfortable in a different way than days one and two. It's not panic anymore. It's emptiness.

Your brain has stopped screaming for stimulation but hasn't yet remembered how to find reward in normal activities. Everything feels flat. Boring. Pointless. You're not in pain exactly, but you're not experiencing pleasure either.

This is called anhedonia. The temporary inability to feel joy. It's a normal part of dopamine receptor upregulation.

Your task during days three through seven is to keep going despite this flatness. You're in the trough. The only way out is through.

Day three usually brings a false sense of confidence. The worst is over, you think. You've made it through the acute withdrawal. You've got this.

Then day four hits and you realize you don't got this. Day four is often worse than day two because the determination that carried you through the first 72 hours has worn off and the benefits haven't appeared yet.

You're tired of feeling uncomfortable. You're tired of boring activities. You're tired of sitting with yourself. Your brain starts questioning whether this is worth it.

This is the make-or-break moment. Most people who survive days one and two quit during days four through six. They decide the reset isn't working because they don't feel better yet.

But neuroplasticity doesn't work that fast. Receptors upregulate and old neural associations weaken, but you won't feel it until enough biological change accumulates. You can't rush it. You can only not interrupt it.

Think of it like planting seeds. Days one through seven are spent preparing the soil and planting. Nothing visible is happening above ground. But underground, roots are forming. You just can't see them yet.

During this phase, your job is to trust the process even when you can't see results.

Specific challenges and solutions for days three through seven:

> **Neuroscience fact**
> During the first week of detox, dopamine receptor density begins to rise again—but the subjective sense of pleasure lags behind by several days. (Neuropsychopharmacology, 2018)

The flatness problem. Nothing brings you joy. Your solution isn't to seek more stimulation. It's to do rewarding activities anyway, even though they don't feel rewarding yet. Read even though it's boring. Exercise even though it feels pointless. Create even though you feel no inspiration. You're not doing these things because they feel good. You're doing them to rebuild the pathways that make them feel good.

The "this isn't working" doubt. Around day five, you'll be convinced you're wasting your time. Your solution is to review your baseline metrics. You're not trying to feel great by day five. You're trying to begin the biological process of recovery. That process has a timeline that doesn't care about your impatience.

The productivity pressure. You might feel like you should be accomplishing huge amounts of work now that you're not distracted. You probably won't be. Your brain is using resources to heal. Productivity comes later. For now, just maintain the reset.

The social pressure. People will want things from you. Responses to messages. Attention. Engagement. Let them wait. Your reset is more important than their convenience.

By day seven, something subtle but significant happens. You start having moments of mental clarity. Brief windows where your thoughts feel organized instead of scattered. These moments are fleeting, maybe lasting only a few minutes, but they're proof that your brain is healing.

You might sit down to work on something and realize twenty minutes have passed without you thinking about your phone. You might have a conversation and actually be present instead of planning your next distraction. You might wake up one morning and the first thought isn't about checking notifications.

These small wins matter enormously. They're evidence that the reset is working even when you can't feel the full benefits yet.

Document these moments. Write them down. When doubt hits again on day eight or nine, you'll need proof that progress is happening.

The breakthrough at the end of this phase isn't dramatic. It's not like a switch flips and suddenly everything is better. It's more like fog slowly lifting. You can't pinpoint the exact moment visibility improved, but looking back, you realize you can see further than you could before.

Days three through seven are about endurance. You're not trying to feel good. You're trying to not quit while your brain does the invisible work of healing.

Stay in the gap. The breakthrough is coming.

Days 8-14: Rebuilding Reward Pathways

Week two is where things get interesting. The acute discomfort has mostly passed. The flatness is starting to lift. And for the first time since you started, you'll have moments that feel genuinely good.

Not constantly. Not even frequently. But occasionally, you'll engage in an activity and feel actual satisfaction from it. This is your reward system coming back online.

Your task during days eight through fourteen is to deliberately strengthen these new reward pathways. Every time you feel satisfaction from a healthy activity, you're reinforcing the neural connections that make that activity rewarding. You're literally rewiring your brain.

This phase is less about endurance and more about intention. You're not just avoiding bad behaviors anymore. You're actively building good ones.

Day eight typically brings noticeable improvement in focus. You might work for 45 minutes straight without your attention drifting. This is huge compared to the 15-minute maximum you probably had before the reset. Your brain is remembering how to sustain attention.

> **Stat insight**
> By the second week of a digital fast, dopamine receptor availability can increase by up to 15%, improving motivation and focus stability. (Translational Psychiatry, 2018)

This improvement isn't consistent yet. Some days you'll focus well. Other days you'll struggle. That's normal. Recovery isn't linear.

During this week, start testing your focus capacity. Set a timer for 60 minutes and work on something important without any distractions. Not because you have to, but because you want to measure progress. How far can you push before resistance appears?

When I hit day nine of my first reset, I worked for 90 minutes without checking anything. I didn't even think about my phone until the timer went off. That experience was proof that my brain was capable of focus again. It hadn't felt capable of that in years.

Days nine and ten often bring a surge of energy. After a week of biological recovery, your body has resources it didn't have before. Sleep is deeper. Mornings feel clearer. The background mental fog that you didn't even realize was there starts dissipating.

Use this energy deliberately. Don't waste it on busy work. Focus it on one meaningful project that you've been avoiding. Make real progress. Complete something.

The satisfaction you feel from genuine accomplishment during this phase is different from anything you've felt in a long time. It's not the quick hit of dopamine from a notification. It's deeper, more lasting, more real.

This is what your reward system was designed to respond to. Actual achievement. Real progress. Meaningful work. Your brain is remembering what that feels like.

> **Practical cue**
> At the end of each day, write down one task that felt genuinely satisfying. Re-reading that list builds visible proof that your brain is learning to enjoy substance again.

Day eleven often brings overconfidence. You feel good, focus is improving, and you start thinking maybe you can ease up on the restrictions. Maybe you can check social media just once. Maybe the reset worked and you don't need to continue.

Don't fall for this. Day eleven overconfidence has destroyed more resets than any other single factor. You're feeling better because you're doing the reset, not because you've completed it. Stopping now means losing all progress and starting over.

Your dopamine receptors are upregulating but they're not fully recovered. Reintroduce high-stimulation activities now and you'll crash hard. Worse, you'll have taught your brain that it can manipulate you into quitting early.

Stay the course. The benefits you're experiencing are just the beginning.

Days twelve through fourteen are about building positive momentum. Each day should include at least one activity where you deliberately practice sustained focus. Reading for an hour. Working on a project for 90 minutes. Having a conversation without distraction.

Track how these sessions feel. Rate your mental clarity, your ease of focus, your satisfaction afterwards. You're gathering evidence that your brain is healing.

During this week, you'll also notice changes in how you experience downtime. Empty moments don't immediately trigger the urge to seek stimulation. You can stand in line without reaching for your phone. You can sit in silence without discomfort.

This tolerance for understimulation is one of the most important developments of week two. It means your brain's dopamine baseline has lowered enough that normal life doesn't feel boring anymore.

Practical focus-building exercises for days eight through fourteen:

The focus ladder. Start with 30-minute work sessions. When comfortable, move to 45, then 60, then 90 minutes. Time each session. Log the duration. Rate your focus quality 1-10 afterwards.

Single-tasking practice. One task for a set period. Timer on. No switches. If your mind wanders to other tasks, write them down for later. Track how many times you maintain single focus successfully.

Analog activities. One hour per day on completely non-digital activities. Cook, draw, build, garden. Log which activities provide the most satisfaction.

Conversation depth. One 30-minute conversation where you're completely present. No phone. Rate your presence level afterwards.

Completion practice. Finish one thing per day. Book chapter, project section, anything. Mark each completion. Watch the list grow.

By the end of week two, you should notice measurable improvements in your baseline metrics. Your focus duration should be longer. Your mental clarity ratings should be higher. Your satisfaction with days should increase.

If you're not seeing improvements by day fourteen, something in your protocol needs adjustment. You might not be strict enough with elimination activities. You might not be implementing enough replacement activities. Review your trigger matrix and tighten your boundaries.

But most people who make it to day fourteen see clear progress. The fog is lifting. Focus is returning. Life is starting to feel manageable again.

Week two is where you stop just surviving the reset and start actively rebuilding your cognitive function. This is where the real work happens.

Days 15-21: Momentum Building

Week three is when everything starts clicking. The scattered pieces begin assembling into coherent patterns. Focus that required intense effort in week two starts feeling more natural. Activities that felt unrewarding in week one now provide genuine satisfaction.

This is momentum. This is your brain operating closer to how it was designed to function.

Your primary task during days fifteen through twenty-one is to protect and amplify this momentum. You're building flywheel energy. Each good day makes the next day easier. Each focused work session makes the next one more accessible.

But momentum cuts both ways. One major slip-up can destroy weeks of progress. So while you're feeling better, you can't get sloppy about boundaries.

Day fifteen typically brings a qualitative shift in how focus feels. Instead of forcing yourself to concentrate, you find yourself naturally drawn into work. Flow states become possible again. You might sit down for what you think will be a 30-minute session and look up 90 minutes later, surprised that time passed so quickly.

This is what healthy dopamine function feels like. Tasks that are challenging but meaningful naturally capture your attention because your reward system recognizes them as worthwhile.

When you experience this kind of focus, pay attention to what enabled it. What time of day was it? What was your mental state beforehand? What environmental conditions were present? Replicate these conditions deliberately.

For me, morning focus sessions after light exercise and before any digital input became my highest-quality work time. I discovered this by accident on day sixteen and then engineered it into my routine going forward.

Days sixteen and seventeen often bring the first real test of your reset: something stressful happens. A work crisis, a relationship conflict, bad news. Your first instinct will be to cope the way you used to, by seeking digital distraction.

Don't. Execute your Emergency Protocol.

Getting through one stressful situation without breaking proves to your brain that you don't need digital escape to survive difficult emotions. This proof is essential for long-term change.

Day eighteen often brings what I call the "abundance feeling." For the first time in possibly years, you feel like you have enough time. Your days feel spacious instead of compressed. You're accomplishing more in less time because you're not hemorrhaging attention to distractions.

This feeling is intoxicating. Enjoy it, but stay vigilant. Abundance can breed complacency. You might think you can afford to check social media "just once" because you have time to spare.

You don't. The abundance you're feeling exists because you're protecting your attention. The moment you stop protecting it, the abundance disappears.

Days nineteen through twenty-one are about consolidating gains. Each day should include:

One long focus session where you test the upper limits of your current capacity. How long can you work before attention wavers? Push slightly beyond your comfortable limit. This is how you expand capacity over time.

One completion. Finish something meaningful every day. It doesn't have to be huge. Complete a chapter, finish a workout, have a full conversation. Train your brain that you're someone who completes things now.

One moment of deliberate understimulation. Spend fifteen minutes doing nothing. Just sitting. Being bored. This continues recalibrating your dopamine baseline downward.

One connection. Talk to someone you care about with full presence. Your relationships have probably suffered during your years of scattered attention. Rebuilding them matters.

By day twenty, you should be noticing changes that others can see. People might comment that you seem more present, more calm, more focused. These external observations confirm what you're feeling internally.

> **Interesting fact**
> After three weeks of reduced digital stimulation, brain scans show increased activity in the default mode network, the system tied to reflection, memory, and self-awareness—signs that focus and presence are stabilizing. (NeuroImage, 2019)

The momentum you're building in week three isn't just about productivity. It's about rediscovering what it feels like to be fully alive in your own life. Not halfway checked out, not mentally somewhere else, but actually here, experiencing your actual existence.

This might sound dramatic, but it's accurate. Digital overstimulation had disconnected you from reality. You were physically present but mentally absent. The momentum of week three is you reconnecting.

Protect this momentum fiercely. You've worked too hard to get here to throw it away on impulse.

Days 22-30: Integration and Testing

The final nine days are about proving to yourself that what you've built is sustainable. You're not just temporarily improving. You're establishing a new normal.

This phase requires a different kind of discipline than the earlier ones. You're no longer fighting acute withdrawal or pushing through flatness. You're maintaining something good against the subtle pull of old patterns.

Days twenty-two through twenty-five are about stress testing your reset. Deliberately put yourself in situations that used to trigger phone checking or scrolling. See if your new patterns hold under pressure.

Wait in a long line without your phone. Experience awkward silence in a social situation without reaching for distraction. Face boredom without immediately filling it. Hit a frustrating problem without escaping into digital comfort.

If you handle these situations without breaking your reset, your new patterns are integrating into your actual life. If you struggle, you know where you still have work to do.

I tested my reset by attending a social event where I knew almost no one and deliberately leaving my phone in my car. The old me would have checked it every ten minutes to escape social discomfort. The new me was able to engage with strangers, tolerate awkward moments, and actually enjoy the experience.

That test proved something important: my reset wasn't just working in controlled conditions. It was working in real life.

Days twenty-six and twenty-seven often bring what I call the "forgetting phase." You go hours without thinking about the reset.

You're not consciously avoiding your phone or forcing focus. You're just living, and the improved patterns are happening automatically.

This is the goal. When you stop having to actively resist temptation and start naturally preferring healthy behaviors, your reset has succeeded. You're not white-knuckling anymore. You've changed the defaults.

But don't mistake this for being "cured." Your dopamine system is much healthier than it was 26 days ago, but it's not invincible. Reintroduce high-stimulation activities carelessly and you'll regress quickly.

Days twenty-eight through thirty are about planning what comes next. Your 30-day reset is ending. Now what?

You have three options:

Option one is to maintain strict boundaries indefinitely. This works for people who recognize they can't handle any exposure to previous triggers without spiraling. Like an alcoholic choosing permanent abstinence, you decide certain activities are permanently off-limits.

Option two is controlled reintroduction. You carefully add back some eliminated activities but with strict limits. Maybe you allow social media for 20 minutes on Sundays only. Maybe you permit Netflix but only one pre-chosen show per week. This requires honest self-assessment about whether you can maintain boundaries.

Option three is periodic resets. You return to normal life but schedule quarterly 7-day resets to prevent dopamine creep. This assumes you can catch yourself before complete dysregulation happens again.

I personally use a combination of option two and three. Some high-stimulation activities remain permanently eliminated because I know I can't handle them responsibly. Others I allow in limited, structured ways. And I do a 7-day reset every three months as maintenance.

The final three days of your reset should include reviewing your baseline metrics. How do your current numbers compare to day zero?

Your phone unlocks should be dramatically lower. Your focus duration should be significantly longer. Your mental clarity and satisfaction ratings should be markedly higher. Your completion rate should show you're actually finishing things now.

Write these comparisons down. This is your proof that the reset worked. When doubt creeps in during month two or three, when you wonder if it was all placebo, you'll have objective evidence that real change occurred.

Day thirty isn't about celebration. It's about commitment. You're committing to protecting what you've built. You're committing to never going back to the scattered, overstimulated state you were in before.

This commitment might mean permanent changes to your relationship with technology. It definitely means ongoing vigilance. Your dopamine system can be hijacked again if you're not careful. The same mechanisms that created the problem are still out there, still trying to capture your attention.

But now you know how to recognize the trap. You know how to escape it. And you know what your brain is capable of when it's not being hijacked.

The final lesson of the 30-day reset: this is not about perfection. You will have slip-ups. You will have days where focus is harder. You will occasionally fall into old patterns. That's normal. That's being human.

What matters is not whether you stumble. What matters is whether you have the awareness to notice when you're stumbling and the tools to correct course before you completely regress.

Your 30-day reset gave you both. Now you have to use them.

A Minute That Makes a Difference

Small actions often carry the most weight. If these pages have helped you pause, reflect, or see things differently, you already know how powerful awareness can be. You can extend that impact in under a minute. By leaving a short, honest review, you help others who are still struggling to find focus and direction.

Your words can help:

- One more person feel less trapped by distraction
- One more reader rediscover motivation
- One more life shift toward clarity and purpose

It doesn't take much. Even a single line about what resonated with you or what surprised you can guide someone else.

I read every review personally and I'm thankful for them all, whether positive or critical. Each one helps me grow and ensures these ideas reach those who truly need them.

Thank you for taking the time to make a small difference that lasts.

Andy.

Scan to leave a review

Chapter 6:
Reclaiming Your Focus

"Concentrate all your thoughts upon the work in hand. The sun's rays do not burn until brought to a focus." Alexander Graham Bell

You've completed the reset. Your dopamine receptors are functional again. The fog has lifted. You can think clearly for the first time in years.

Now comes the next challenge: turning that recovered capacity into actual skill.

Having a healthy dopamine system is necessary, but not sufficient. You still need to learn how to use it effectively.

This chapter is about building focus as a practiced ability, not just a biological state. It's about transforming your recovered attention span from potential into performance.

The difference matters. Plenty of people complete dopamine resets and feel better, then wonder why they're still not as productive as they expected. The answer is simple: they restored their hardware but never upgraded their software.

Focus is a skill. Like any skill, it requires deliberate practice, progressive challenge, and specific techniques. Your brain now has the capacity to focus. This chapter teaches you how to actually do it.

The Art of Deep Work

Deep work is the ability to focus without distraction on a cognitively demanding task. It's the state where you produce your best work, solve your hardest problems, and create your most valuable output.

Most people have forgotten what deep work feels like. They've spent so long in shallow work mode, constantly interrupted and partially attentive, that they think that's normal.

It's not. Deep work is your natural state when your dopamine system isn't hijacked and you create the right conditions.

The first principle of deep work is this: it requires deliberate entry. You don't accidentally fall into deep focus. You intentionally create it.

Start by defining what deep work means for your specific situation. For a writer, it's producing new words without editing. For a programmer, it's solving complex problems without checking documentation constantly. For a strategist, it's thinking through implications without jumping to execution.

Whatever your work is, identify the activity that requires your highest level of cognitive function. That's your deep work. Everything else is shallow work or maintenance.

Block your day: a few sacred deep-work windows and separate shallow blocks for maintenance tasks. Enter deliberately with one specific goal, remove all optional inputs, and build in a 5-minute cooldown to exit the session properly.

Deep work requires specific environmental conditions. Your workspace during deep work blocks should contain only what's necessary for the task.

Silence is often optimal for deep work, but some people focus better with ambient sound. White noise, nature sounds, or instrumental music can mask distracting environmental noise without creating new distractions. Test different conditions and find what works for your brain.

Temperature matters more than people realize. Too hot and you get drowsy. Too cold and you're distracted by discomfort. Find your optimal temperature and maintain it during deep work sessions.

> **Focus stat**
> After just 20 minutes of interrupted work, it can take your brain over 23 minutes to regain full concentration. (University of California, Irvine, 2014)

Lighting affects cognitive function. Bright, natural light is ideal. Dim lighting signals to your brain it's time to wind down, which works against deep focus. If natural light isn't available, use full-spectrum bulbs that mimic daylight.

Your posture influences your mental state. Slouching correlates with lower focus and energy. Sitting upright or standing signals alertness to your brain. Don't underestimate the mind-body connection.

Before entering a deep work block, prepare everything you'll need. Water, notes, reference materials. Once you start, you don't stop to get things. Preparation eliminates excuses for breaking focus.

Set a clear goal for each deep work session. Not "work on project" but "complete section three of the proposal" or "solve the authentication bug" or "write 1000 words of chapter six." Specific goals focus your attention and provide clear endpoints.

During the session, expect your attention to waver. It will. Especially at first. When it does, don't judge yourself. Simply notice the distraction and redirect attention back to the task. This is the practice. Noticing and redirecting, over and over.

Each successful redirection strengthens your focus muscle. Each time you catch yourself drifting and bring yourself back, you're training your brain that you control attention, not the other way around.

The end of a deep work session matters as much as the beginning. Don't immediately jump into shallow work. Give yourself five minutes to transition. Close your eyes, take deep breaths, let your brain shift modes gradually.

This transition time prevents the mental whiplash of moving from deep concentration to scattered attention. It also creates a clear boundary that trains your brain to recognize when focus time is over.

Deep work isn't something you do occasionally when you have time. It's something you schedule and protect like the most important appointments of your day. Because they are.

Training Your Attention Span

Your attention span right now is probably longer than it was before your reset, but it's not as long as it could be. Like physical endurance, attention endurance can be trained.

Most people assume attention span is fixed. You either have it or you don't. This is completely wrong. Attention is trainable through progressive challenge.

Think of it like running. Someone who hasn't run in years can't complete a marathon on their first attempt. They start with a mile, then two, then five, building capacity gradually over months.

Attention works the same way. If you haven't focused deeply in years, you can't suddenly work for three hours straight. You start where you are and progressively extend.

This is your post-reset, 4-week attention plan: 25→35→45→60 minutes with 5-minute breaks, logging redirections per session and perceived output quality. It's the same ladder principle from Chapter 5, now formalized as a progression you can repeat quarterly.

Week one, work in 25-minute blocks. Set a timer. Focus on one task until the timer sounds. Take a five-minute break. Repeat.

During the 25 minutes, your only job is to keep attention on the task. When your mind wanders, which it will, notice and redirect. Count how many times you successfully redirect. That number is your focus score for the session.

Week two, extend to 35-minute blocks. Same process. Timer, task, break. The extra ten minutes will feel challenging at first. That challenge is how you know you're training the skill.

Week three, move to 45-minute blocks. By now, you should notice that the redirecting happens less frequently. Your attention is stabilizing. The neural pathways for sustained focus are strengthening.

> **Brain fact**
> Focused practice literally thickens the brain's prefrontal cortex—the area responsible for attention control and decision-making. (Harvard Gazette, 2018)

Week four, attempt 60-minute blocks. This is a significant threshold. Most cognitive work can be completed in 60-minute sessions. Getting comfortable at this duration gives you a solid baseline for productive work.

Beyond week four, you can push toward 90-minute blocks if your work demands it. But understand that 90 minutes is close to the upper limit for most people's optimal focus capacity. Going beyond that usually results in diminishing returns.

The key principle is progressive overload. You're constantly pushing slightly beyond your comfortable capacity, forcing your attention span to expand. But you're not jumping so far ahead that you fail and get discouraged.

Track your progress. Keep a log of focus duration, number of redirections needed, and quality of work produced. This data shows you whether your training is working and where you need to adjust.

When I started this training, I could barely manage 25 minutes before my attention completely disintegrated. By week six, I was comfortably working in 90-minute blocks and producing better work than I had in years.

The improvement wasn't linear. Some days were harder than others. Some weeks felt like plateaus. But the overall trend was clear: consistent practice was expanding my attention capacity.

During training, expect discomfort. The point where your attention wants to break is exactly the point where training happens. Pushing through that discomfort, even for an extra two minutes, is what expands capacity.

> **Pro tip**
> End your focus block before you're completely drained. Stopping with a bit of energy left trains your brain to *want* to return next time.

Think of it like lifting weights. The last few reps, when your muscles are fatigued and you want to quit, are the ones that actually build strength. Attention training works the same way. The moments when focus is hard are the moments when growth happens.

But also respect your limits. If you're genuinely exhausted, if you've been pushing hard all week, if your brain is giving clear signals that it needs rest, listen. Overtraining destroys progress just as much as undertraining.

Rest days matter. Your brain needs time to consolidate the neural changes you're creating through practice. Taking one or two days per week with no intense focus training actually improves long-term results.

As your attention span extends, you'll notice secondary benefits. Decision-making improves because you can hold multiple factors in mind simultaneously. Problem-solving gets easier because you can think through complex chains of reasoning without losing the thread.

Conversations become more satisfying because you can actually listen to someone for five minutes without your mind wandering to your next task. Reading becomes enjoyable again because you can follow a narrative or argument without constantly checking how many pages are left.

These benefits compound. Each improvement in attention capacity makes everything else in your life work better. It's one of the highest-leverage skills you can develop.

Mastering Monotasking

Multitasking is a myth. Your brain doesn't do two cognitively demanding tasks simultaneously. It switches rapidly between them, and every switch carries a cost.

That cost is called attention residue. When you shift from task A to task B, part of your attention remains stuck on task A. You're never fully present with task B because your brain is still processing the previous task.

The more you switch, the more residue accumulates, until you're not fully present with anything. You're scattered across multiple incomplete thoughts, producing subpar results on everything.

Monotasking is the antidote. One task. Full attention. Nothing else until it's complete or the session ends.

This sounds simple. It's not. Your brain will resist monotasking because it's been trained to switch tasks whenever things get difficult or boring. You'll need to actively practice staying with one thing.

Start by identifying your biggest multitasking triggers. For most people, these are:

> **Pro tip**
> End each focus block before exhaustion hits—quitting on a high note keeps your brain eager to re-enter deep work.

Getting stuck on a problem and immediately switching to something easier instead of thinking through the difficulty.

Receiving a notification and switching to check it even though you're in the middle of something important.

Feeling bored with a task and seeking variety by starting something new before finishing the current thing.

Feeling anxious about another task and switching to it prematurely instead of completing what you're already doing.

Write down your specific triggers. When do you switch tasks? What emotion precedes the switch? What thought pattern justifies it?

Once you know your triggers, you can catch them before they control your behavior. The moment you feel the urge to switch tasks, pause. Take three breaths. Ask yourself: "Am I switching because this task is complete, or because I'm avoiding difficulty?"

If you're avoiding difficulty, stay with the current task for ten more minutes. Usually, the difficulty resolves once you push through the resistance. The urge to switch was just your brain seeking easier dopamine.

If the task truly is stuck and you need different information or perspective, that's a legitimate reason to switch. But schedule it. Don't switch impulsively. Finish a clear stopping point with the current task, then deliberately move to the next.

One powerful monotasking technique is the "capture and continue" method. When a thought about a different task pops into your mind during focused work, don't follow it. Instead, write it down in two words on a capture sheet, then immediately return attention to your current task.

The two-word limit is crucial. If you write full thoughts, you're still task-switching mentally. Two words is enough to capture the idea so you don't lose it, but not enough to pull you into thinking about it.

> **Quick practice**
> When your mind drifts, label the distraction in one word—*email, snack, scroll*. Naming it breaks the loop and restores control in seconds.

At the end of your focus session, review your capture sheet. Most of those thoughts that felt urgent in the moment are either irrelevant or can wait. The few that are actually important, you handle in your next shallow work block.

This method satisfies your brain's anxiety about forgetting things while keeping you locked into monotasking. You're not ignoring other tasks. You're strategically deferring them.

Batch email, meetings, and calls into tight windows; protect large, continuous blocks for monotasking.

For creative work, monotasking is especially critical. You can't write well while also answering messages. You can't design effectively while also monitoring chat channels. Creative flow requires complete immersion, which is impossible when you're task-switching.

I used to pride myself on handling multiple projects simultaneously. In reality, I was producing mediocre work on everything because I was never fully present with anything. When I committed to monotasking, the quality of my output jumped dramatically. I wasn't smarter. I was just fully engaged.

The hardest part of monotasking is the emotional discomfort it creates. When you stay with one difficult task instead of switching to something easier, you feel the full weight of the difficulty. There's no escape.

That discomfort is productive. It's where problem-solving happens. It's where creativity emerges. It's where you develop actual skill at your work. But it requires tolerating the discomfort instead of constantly seeking relief through task-switching.

Practice tolerating ten more minutes of difficulty before switching tasks. Then fifteen. Then twenty. You're training your brain that difficulty isn't dangerous and doesn't require immediate escape.

Over time, monotasking becomes your default mode instead of multitasking. You stop feeling the urge to switch tasks constantly. Your brain recognizes that staying focused produces better results with less stress.

That's the paradox of monotasking. It feels slower in the moment but it's actually much faster overall. One hour of focused monotasking accomplishes more than four hours of scattered multitasking.

Building Your Concentration Muscle

Concentration is like a muscle. Use it and it gets stronger. Neglect it and it atrophies. Your reset gave you a functional muscle again. Now you need to deliberately strengthen it.

The concentration muscle has two components: capacity and control. Capacity is how long you can focus. Control is how precisely you can direct attention where you want it.

You've been building capacity through attention span training. Now let's work on control.

Attention control means being able to place your focus on one thing and keep it there despite distractions. Internal distractions like wandering thoughts. External distractions like noise or movement.

Most people have weak attention control. Their focus drifts to whatever is loudest, brightest, or most emotionally charged. They don't control where attention goes. They react to whatever captures it.

Training attention control starts with noticing where your attention is right now. Throughout your day, pause every thirty minutes and ask: "What am I paying attention to?" Often, you'll discover you're not paying attention to anything specific. You're just scattered.

This awareness practice is the foundation of control. You can't direct attention until you know where it currently is.

The next level is deliberate direction. Choose something to focus on. A physical object in your environment, your breathing, a specific thought. Place your attention on it fully for sixty seconds.

Your attention will wander. Probably within ten seconds. That's normal. When you notice it wandering, gently bring it

> **Practice tip**
> Each time your focus drifts and you bring it back, count that as a *rep*. Ten mindful redirections a day will do more for your concentration than one "perfect" session.

back to your chosen focus point. Do this as many times as necessary for sixty seconds.

Count how many redirections you need. That number represents your current attention control level. With practice, the number of redirections decreases. You're strengthening control.

Do this exercise once per day. It takes two minutes total. The results compound over weeks.

A more advanced control exercise involves working in a mildly distracting environment and maintaining focus despite the distractions. Not a chaotic environment that makes focus impossible. A mildly distracting one that challenges your control.

Maybe a coffee shop with ambient conversation. Maybe your home office with family members moving around. The goal is to practice holding focus while distractions exist, rather than only being able to focus in perfect silence.

> **Neuroscience fact**
> Regular mindfulness or attention training can increase gray matter density in brain regions linked to focus and emotional regulation after just 8 weeks. (Psychiatry Research: Neuroimaging, 2011)

This trains your brain that focus isn't dependent on perfect conditions. You can maintain concentration even when things aren't ideal. This resilience is valuable in real-world situations where you can't always control your environment.

When I started practicing focus in mildly distracting environments, my attention was constantly pulled away. Over time, I learned to acknowledge distractions without following them. A loud sound would happen, I'd notice it, then immediately return focus to my work.

That ability to notice without engaging is the essence of attention control. Distractions don't disappear. You just stop being controlled by them.

Physical practices also strengthen concentration. Meditation is obvious and effective. Ten minutes per day of focusing on your breath and redirecting when your mind wanders builds the same neural pathways you use for work focus.

But physical exercise works too. When you're running and you want to stop but you maintain pace for two more minutes, you're training the same mental muscle. When you're lifting weights and you complete three more reps despite fatigue, you're building concentration.

Any activity that requires sustained effort despite discomfort strengthens your ability to maintain focus during cognitive difficulty. The muscle is the same. The context is different.

> **Quick exercise**
> Pick one routine task—making coffee, brushing your teeth, tying your shoes and do it with *complete* attention for 60 seconds. Training focus in the ordinary strengthens it for the complex.

Reading physical books is excellent concentration training. No hyperlinks to click. No notifications to check. Just sustained attention on one linear narrative or argument for extended time.

If you can't read for thirty minutes without breaking focus, your concentration muscle needs work.

Playing a musical instrument trains concentration through the requirement for complete presence. One mistake and you have to start over. This immediate feedback loop strengthens focus control rapidly.

Even cooking a complex recipe builds concentration. Following multiple steps, managing timing, staying present with the process. Any activity that punishes distraction and rewards focus will strengthen the muscle.

The key is consistency. Sporadic intense practice is less effective than regular moderate practice. Ten minutes of daily concentration training beats three hours on Sunday followed by six days of nothing.

Your concentration muscle also needs rest. If you've done deep focus work for three hours, your concentration is depleted. Pushing for a fourth hour produces diminishing returns and risks burning out the muscle.

Learn to recognize mental fatigue. Your attention starts drifting more frequently. Redirecting becomes harder. Tasks take longer. These are signs you've exhausted your concentration capacity for now.

When that happens, rest. Do shallow work that doesn't require focus. Take a walk. Have a meal. Give your brain time to recover. Concentration capacity replenishes with rest, just like physical strength.

Most people try to power through concentration fatigue with willpower. This doesn't work. You just produce worse results while exhausting yourself. Better to recognize fatigue early and rest strategically.

With consistent training, your concentration muscle gets stronger. You can focus longer, direct attention more precisely, and maintain control in challenging conditions. This isn't a minor improvement in life quality. It's transformative.

Strong concentration is the foundation of expertise in any field. You can't become skilled at something you can't focus on consistently. Every expert is first and foremost someone who can concentrate deeply.

Build the muscle. The rest follows.

The Morning 90-Minute Rule

The first 90 minutes after you wake up are the most valuable 90 minutes of your day for cognitive work. Your brain is fresh, your willpower is full, and your dopamine sensitivity is at its natural peak.

Most people waste these 90 minutes on low-value activities. Checking email, scrolling news, engaging with messages, consuming content. They're spending premium mental currency on things that could happen any time.

This is backwards. The first 90 minutes should be protected for your most important work. The work that requires your highest level of cognitive function. The work that will still matter in five years.

The rule is simple: no input for the first 90 minutes. No checking anything. No consuming anything. Only creating or thinking deeply. This single practice will transform your productivity more than any other technique.

Here's what this looks like practically:

You wake up. You don't check your phone. You follow your morning routine. Exercise, shower, coffee, whatever. But no digital input of any kind.

Ninety minutes after waking up, not ninety minutes after getting to your desk, you sit down for deep work. After sleep, neurotransmitters and memory consolidation peak—spend that fresh state on creation before any input.

You work on the one thing that matters most. Not urgent emails. Not administrative tasks. The thing that if you accomplished only this today, the day would be successful.

During this 90-minute window, you can accomplish more high-quality work than in the entire rest of the day combined. Because your brain is operating at peak capacity without depletion or distraction.

> **Pro tip**
> Before your 90-minute block, write tomorrow's single top task on paper. When you wake, you won't negotiate—you'll just begin.

After 90 minutes, you can handle input. Check email, respond to messages, engage with the world. But you've already done your most important work. Everything else is secondary.

But most people will resist this rule because they're addicted to morning input. Nothing that happened overnight requires your immediate attention in the first 90 minutes. Everything else can wait.

I fought this rule for months before trying it. The first morning felt unbearable. I was convinced something urgent needed my attention immediately. It didn't. Nothing bad happened by waiting 90 minutes.

By the second week, the anxiety disappeared. By the fourth week, I couldn't imagine starting my day any other way. The output I was producing in those morning 90 minutes was better than anything I'd created in years.

Some variations on this rule work for different situations:

If you have young children who need care immediately upon waking, the 90 minutes starts after their morning needs are handled. The principle holds: 90 minutes of deep work before any digital input.

If you have a job that requires immediate responsiveness, negotiate this boundary explicitly with your team. Most jobs that people think require immediate responsiveness actually don't. The expectation was created by behavior patterns, not genuine necessity.

If you're not a morning person and your peak cognitive time is afternoon or evening, apply the 90-minute rule to whenever you naturally wake up fully. The principle is protecting your peak state, not forcing morning productivity.

The key is identifying when your brain is freshest and protecting that time ruthlessly. For most people, it's morning. For some, it's afternoon. Know your pattern and structure around it.

What should you work on during your protected 90 minutes? It should be important, not urgent. It should require deep thinking, not shallow execution. It should contribute to long-term goals, not just daily maintenance.

> **Quick stat**
> People who start their day with focused, offline work report a 53% higher likelihood of entering flow states later that same day.
> (University of Toronto, 2020)

For a writer, it's producing new words. For a developer, it's solving complex architecture problems. For a strategist, it's thinking through implications and planning. For an entrepreneur, it's working on the business, not in the business.

Whatever your field, you know what your highest-value work is. That's what belongs in the morning 90 minutes.

One final critical point: the morning 90-minute rule doesn't mean you only work 90 minutes per day. It means you protect those specific 90 minutes for peak work. The rest of your day can include other work, but those 90 minutes are sacred.

This practice requires discipline, especially at first. Your brain will invent urgent reasons why you need to check email immediately. Push through. After two weeks, the new pattern becomes normal. After four weeks, you'll wonder how you ever worked any other way.

Because you'll have proof. You'll see the results in your actual output. The projects you complete, the problems you solve, the work you produce. All coming from those protected 90 minutes of peak cognitive function.

The morning 90-minute rule isn't about being productive all day. It's about being strategically productive during your most valuable time. Master this, and everything else becomes easier.

Chapter 7:
Rebuilding Real Motivation

"People often say that motivation doesn't last. Well, neither does bathing. That's why we recommend it daily." Zig Ziglar

Your dopamine system is reset. Your focus capacity is rebuilt. You can concentrate for hours when you choose to.

So why aren't you choosing to?

This is the question that haunts people after successful resets. They have the ability to do the work, but they're not feeling driven to do it. The internal push that used to propel them forward is missing.

Here's what most people misunderstand: motivation isn't a feeling you wait for. It's a system you build. The dopamine reset removed artificial sources of motivation. Now you need to cultivate authentic ones.

The difference between people who sustain their reset long-term and people who gradually slide back isn't willpower. It's that the successful ones rebuilt their motivation architecture from the ground up.

This chapter shows you how.

Discovering Intrinsic vs Extrinsic Drive

There are two types of motivation, and confusing them destroys your ability to sustain effort.

Extrinsic motivation comes from outside you. Money, recognition, avoiding punishment, pleasing others, winning competitions. You do the work because of what you'll get or avoid as a result.

Intrinsic motivation comes from inside you. Curiosity, mastery, purpose, enjoyment of the process itself. You do the work because the work itself is rewarding.

Both types are real. Both can drive behavior. But they work through completely different mechanisms, and only one is sustainable long-term.

Extrinsic motivation is powerful but fragile. It works great when the external reward is close and certain. You'll work hard if someone is paying you well or if a deadline is tomorrow. But remove the external pressure and the motivation evaporates instantly.

> **Research insight**
> When people focus on mastery and purpose instead of rewards, their long-term performance rises by over 30%, even with no extra pay. (Journal of Personality and Social Psychology, 2009)

Worse, relying primarily on extrinsic motivation gradually undermines intrinsic motivation. When you do something for external rewards long enough, you start losing interest in the activity itself. It becomes pure transaction. Work for pay. Effort for recognition. Nothing more.

This is called the overjustification effect. External rewards crowd out internal satisfaction. The activity that once brought you joy becomes just another task you do for outcomes.

I watched this happen to my writing. I started because I loved thinking through ideas and expressing them clearly. That was intrinsically rewarding. Then I started getting paid for articles. The money was good. But over time, I stopped writing unless I was getting paid. Writing without a check attached felt pointless.

The external reward had killed the internal motivation. I'd transformed something I loved into something I did only for money.

Intrinsic motivation, on the other hand, is self-sustaining. When you're motivated by curiosity, you don't need external rewards to keep exploring. When you're driven by mastery, improving the skill is reward enough. When you're connected to purpose, doing the work feels meaningful regardless of outcomes.

The challenge is that intrinsic motivation develops more slowly than extrinsic motivation. You can bribe someone to do something immediately. But helping them find internal reasons to care takes time and reflection.

Most people never do this reflection. They just assume motivation means feeling excited about outcomes. When excitement fades, they think their motivation is gone. But they never had sustainable motivation to begin with. They had temporary enthusiasm driven by imagined external rewards.

Building intrinsic motivation requires asking different questions. Not "What will I get from this?" but "What about this activity connects to who I want to become?"

> **Reflection prompt**
> Ask yourself: *Would I still do this if no one ever saw the result?* If the answer's yes, you've found real motivation—not rented enthusiasm.

Not "How will this benefit me?" but "What skills does this develop that I find inherently interesting?"

Not "Who will be impressed?" but "Does this challenge me in ways that feel meaningful?"

These questions reveal whether you have genuine internal reasons to do something, or whether you're just chasing external validation.

For most people post-reset, the answer is uncomfortable. They discover they've been doing things for years without any intrinsic motivation. Their entire work life has been transactional. They do tasks to get outcomes, not because the tasks themselves matter to them.

This realization is valuable. Because once you see that your motivation structure is purely extrinsic, you can start building intrinsic sources deliberately.

The process starts with honest inventory. Look at how you currently spend your time. For each significant activity, ask: "Would I do this if no one paid me and no one knew I was doing it?"

If the answer is no for most activities, you're running on extrinsic fuel. That works until external circumstances change. Then you're stranded without internal drive.

If the answer is yes for at least some activities, you have kernels of intrinsic motivation to build from.

The goal isn't to eliminate all extrinsic motivation. External rewards aren't evil. The goal is to ensure you're not dependent on them. That you have internal sources of drive strong enough to sustain effort even when external rewards are delayed or absent.

When your dopamine system was hijacked, you lost access to both types of motivation. The reset restored your capacity for both. But you need to consciously choose which one to build your life around.

Choose intrinsic. It's harder to develop but infinitely more sustainable.

Creating Meaningful Goals That Pull You Forward

Most goals push you. They're obligations you force yourself toward through discipline and willpower. "I should exercise more." "I need to advance my career." "I have to finish this project."

These goals require constant effort to maintain momentum. Stop pushing and you stop moving. That's exhausting.

Better goals pull you. They're visions that naturally draw you forward because they connect to something you genuinely want to become. When goals pull instead of push, effort feels different. You're not forcing yourself. You're choosing to move toward something attractive.

The difference is whether the goal came from authentic desire or external pressure.

Most people set goals based on borrowed desires—what society values, what successful people are supposed to do. These goals might be admirable, but they're not authentic.

This is why New Year's resolutions fail. They're usually push goals dressed up as personal growth. "I should lose weight." "I need to read more." "I have to be more productive." All obligations. Nothing that genuinely excites you.

Pull goals are different. They come from exploring what you're actually curious about. What skills you want to develop regardless of external validation. What kind of person you want to become independent of what others think.

These goals have a different quality. When you think about them, you feel energy instead of obligation. You want to work on them instead of having to work on them.

Finding pull goals requires getting honest about the difference between what you think you should want and what you actually want.

Sit with this question: "If I knew no one would ever see the results, what would I spend my time mastering?"

The answer reveals authentic interests. If you'd still do it in complete privacy, it's probably connected to genuine curiosity or desire for mastery. If you wouldn't, it's likely a borrowed desire.

I discovered through this question that I didn't actually care about growing a massive audience. I thought I should care because that's what content creators are supposed to want. But when I imagined writing with no one reading it, I was still interested. The writing itself pulled me. The audience was nice but not necessary.

That realization changed everything. I stopped optimizing for audience growth and started optimizing for interesting thinking. The work became intrinsically motivating instead of externally driven.

Once you identify pull goals, structure them as identity targets rather than outcome targets. Frame them as who you're becoming, not what you're getting. This shifts the emotional texture completely—you're practicing an identity you want to embody.

Another crucial element of pull goals is connecting them to values beyond yourself. Goals that only serve your own comfort rarely sustain motivation long-term. Goals that contribute to something larger than your individual benefit pull harder.

This doesn't mean you need to save the world. It means asking how your work benefits others or contributes to something you consider important. That connection to broader purpose provides motivation when personal interest fluctuates.

The structure of meaningful goals that pull you forward:

Connected to authentic interest, not borrowed desires. You'd pursue it even if no one knew.

Framed as identity development. Focused on who you're becoming.

Linked to values beyond personal comfort. Contributing to something larger.

Challenging enough to require growth but achievable enough to seem possible. In the zone between boredom and overwhelm.

When goals meet these criteria, motivation stops being something you manufacture through willpower and becomes something that emerges naturally from pursuing things you actually care about.

The Power of Micro-Progress

Big goals inspire. Small progress sustains.

Most people structure their lives around major milestones. They work for months toward a finish line, and their motivation depends on eventually crossing it. This creates a motivation problem: what keeps you going for the months before you reach the milestone?

The answer is micro-progress. Small, visible wins that provide daily evidence you're moving forward.

Your brain responds to progress. Not eventual success. Progress. The feeling that you're getting somewhere. When you experience progress, your brain releases dopamine in a healthy way. This reinforces the behavior and makes you want to continue.

But if progress is invisible for weeks or months, your brain doesn't get that reinforcement. You're working hard with no neurological reward. Eventually, motivation collapses.

The solution is to engineer micro-progress into every day. Not fake progress. Real advancement toward your goals, but measured in small enough increments that you can see it daily.

If your goal is writing a book, measure progress by words written. Five hundred words is achievable daily. Hit that target and you have a clear win. Your brain registers progress. Motivation sustains.

The key is making progress visible. Track it. A simple document. A calendar mark. Physical representation of progress makes the neurological reward stronger.

Another element of micro-progress is celebrating small wins. Most people dismiss small accomplishments as insignificant. They're waiting for the big achievement to feel good about themselves.

This is backwards. Small accomplishments are the only ones that happen frequently enough to provide regular motivation. If you only feel successful when you hit major milestones, you'll spend most of your time feeling unsuccessful.

Instead, acknowledge every meaningful win. Finished a focused work session? That's worth recognition. Completed a difficult task? Notice it. Made progress on a project? Mark it.

This isn't about inflating your ego with false praise. It's about training your brain to associate effort with reward. When your brain learns that working on meaningful things produces good feelings, it wants to work on meaningful things more.

The micro-progress principle also helps with procrastination. When a project feels overwhelming, starting feels impossible. But if you define progress as "open the document and write one sentence," starting becomes achievable.

That one sentence is real progress. Your brain registers it. Often, starting with one sentence leads to writing more. But even if it doesn't, you still made progress. Tomorrow you can make more.

Define your Minimum Viable Progress (MVP) for each goal. The smallest unit of real advancement that counts as a win. Every day you hit that minimum is a success. Mark it on a calendar. The visual accumulation of check marks creates momentum. Extra progress beyond MVP is bonus, but motivation depends on the daily check, not the quantity.

Over weeks and months, minimum viable progress compounds into significant results. The book gets written. The fitness improves. The skill develops. Not through heroic daily efforts, but through consistent small progress that your brain finds rewarding enough to sustain.

Celebrating Without Relapsing

Progress deserves celebration. But how you celebrate determines whether celebration reinforces your new patterns or undermines them.

Most people celebrate achievements by reverting to old behaviors. They work hard all week, then "reward" themselves with exactly the high-dopamine activities they've been avoiding. This creates a contradictory pattern. You're training your brain that doing good work leads to undoing good habits.

The solution is learning to celebrate in ways that align with your reset, not contradict it.

Celebration should enhance your life, not temporarily escape it. When you finish a major project, better celebration involves activities that feel rewarding without being destructive. A nice meal. Time with friends. A long walk somewhere beautiful. Reading a book you've been anticipating.

The test is simple: how do you feel an hour after the celebration? If you feel good, energized, proud of yourself, it was proper celebration. If you feel guilty, sluggish, or like you wasted time, it was a relapse disguised as a reward.

Second principle: celebration should be proportional to achievement. Finishing a 30-minute task doesn't warrant a 3-hour celebration. Big achievements deserve substantial celebration. Small achievements deserve small acknowledgments.

When celebration is proportional, your brain learns accurate associations between effort and reward. Big effort leads to big satisfaction. Small effort leads to small satisfaction. This reinforces motivation appropriately.

Third principle: the best celebrations involve sharing. Humans are social creatures. Achievements feel more meaningful when witnessed and acknowledged by others.

Celebrate by telling someone who cares about your work. Have a conversation about what you accomplished. Let them see your pride. This social dimension of celebration provides dopamine in a healthy, sustainable way.

Fourth principle: build celebration into your process, not just endpoints. Create micro-celebrations for daily progress. Maybe your celebration for hitting your daily goal is enjoying coffee outside instead of at your desk. Maybe it's listening to a favorite song. Maybe it's five minutes of sitting in satisfaction before moving to the next task.

> **Quick check**
> A real reward leaves you clearer, not foggier.
> If you need to recover *from* your celebration, it wasn't one.

These tiny celebrations don't feel dramatic, but they provide the regular reinforcement your brain needs to stay motivated.

One powerful celebration technique is the "done for the day" ritual. When you've completed your meaningful work for the day, have a specific action that marks the transition. Close your laptop with intention. Say "done" out loud. Take a satisfying breath.

This ritual signals to your brain that effort has concluded and satisfaction is appropriate. It creates a clear boundary between working and relaxing.

The final principle: never use high-dopamine activities as rewards. The substances, apps, and behaviors you eliminated during your reset don't become safe just because you accomplished something.

Find rewards that exist outside the addiction cycle. Physical experiences. Real-world pleasures. Human connection. These provide satisfaction without reactivating patterns you've worked hard to break.

Celebration is essential. But celebration only serves you when it reinforces the person you're becoming instead of pulling you back toward the person you've worked to move beyond.

From Forcing to Flowing

The ultimate goal of rebuilding motivation isn't to become better at forcing yourself to do things. It's to reach a state where effort feels natural instead of effortful.

This is flow. Not the psychological state that happens occasionally during peak performance. The broader sense of moving through your work and life without constant internal resistance.

When you're forcing, every action requires a decision. Every task needs motivation manufactured fresh. You're constantly pushing yourself forward through willpower. This is exhausting and unsustainable.

When you're flowing, action emerges from interest and identity rather than obligation. You work on things because you want to, not because you have to. The effort is still real, but the internal resistance is minimal.

The shift from forcing to flowing requires three changes.

First, reduce obligations that don't align with your values. Every commitment you maintain for external reasons creates internal resistance. That resistance drains motivation even when you're working on things you do care about.

You can't flow when you're carrying heavy obligations that don't serve you. The weight slows everything down.

Second, increase time spent on activities that match your intrinsic interests. When you spend more time on intrinsically motivating activities, flow becomes your default state more often. You're not forcing yourself through each day. You're engaging with things that naturally hold your attention.

This requires honest assessment of what you're actually interested in versus what you think you should be interested in. Then restructuring your time to favor the authentic interests.

I shifted from marketing and networking, which drained me, to research and writing,

> **Reflection prompt**
> List one task you constantly have to push yourself to do. Now ask: *If this were part of who I am, not what I do, how would I approach it differently?*

which energized me. The work got easier through alignment, not discipline.

Third, build identity around the person who does this work naturally. When you see yourself as someone who writes daily, writing doesn't require motivation. It's just what you do. The behavior flows from identity.

Identity shapes action more than motivation does. Motivation fluctuates. Identity persists. When your identity aligns with your goals, action becomes natural.

The process of building identity is simple but not easy. You act in accordance with the identity you want to embody, even when it feels artificial at first. Over time, repeated action convinces your brain that this is actually who you are. The identity solidifies. The behavior becomes natural.

The transition from forcing to flowing takes time. You can't flip a switch and suddenly experience effortless action. But you can gradually shift the balance. Each authentic goal added. Each misaligned obligation removed. Each identity-building action taken.

Over months, the internal resistance decreases. More of your life starts feeling natural instead of forced. You still work hard, but the work emerges from who you are rather than who you think you should be.

> **Quick insight**
> Flow doesn't come from doing more—it comes from doing what fits. Every unnecessary obligation you drop frees energy for the work that moves on its own.

That's the difference between sustainable motivation and constant forcing. One comes from alignment with your actual self. The other comes from trying to be someone you're not.

Build the former. Release the latter. Watch how much easier everything becomes when you stop fighting yourself.

Chapter 8:
Managing Relapses and Urges

"Fall seven times, stand up eight." Japanese Proverb

You will relapse. Not maybe. Not if you're weak or undisciplined. You will experience moments where you fall back into old patterns despite your best intentions.

This chapter isn't about preventing relapses. That's impossible. This chapter is about managing them so they become brief detours instead of complete derailments.

The difference between people who maintain their reset long-term and people who gradually slide back isn't that the successful ones never slip. It's that they know how to recover quickly when they do.

Most people treat relapse as binary. You're either perfectly following your reset or you've completely failed. This all-or-nothing thinking is what transforms a minor slip into a full regression.

The reality is more nuanced. Relapses exist on a spectrum. A ten-minute scrolling session isn't the same as a three-day binge. Checking your phone once during a focus session isn't the same as abandoning your boundaries entirely.

Understanding this spectrum and having specific responses for different levels of relapse is what allows you to maintain progress despite imperfection.

Understanding the Relapse Cycle

Relapses don't appear randomly. They follow predictable patterns. When you understand the pattern, you can interrupt it before it

> **Quick insight**
> Feeling an urge doesn't mean you're failing, it means your brain is remembering. The power shift happens when you notice the signal but choose not to obey it.

completes.

The relapse cycle has four stages: trigger, craving, action, and aftermath. Each stage offers an opportunity for intervention.

Stage one is the trigger. Something happens that activates your old neural pathways. A stressful event. An uncomfortable emotion. An environmental cue. The trigger itself isn't the problem. Triggers are unavoidable. What matters is how you respond.

Common triggers: emotions (anxiety, boredom, inadequacy), contexts (bedtime, task transitions), and post-success ("I deserve it" after completing something). Triggers are information, not commands.

The key insight about triggers is that they're just your brain saying "I remember getting dopamine relief in this situation." You can acknowledge that information without acting on it.

Stage two is the craving. The trigger activates a craving for the old behavior. This is where most people think the battle is won or lost. They believe if they can just resist the craving through willpower, they'll be fine.

This is backwards. Fighting cravings through willpower alone is exhausting and often fails. Better to understand that cravings have a predictable arc. They rise, peak, and fall. The entire cycle usually takes ten to fifteen minutes.

If you can observe the craving without acting on it for fifteen minutes, it will diminish on its own. You don't have to defeat it. You just have to outlast it.

The mistake most people make is trying to suppress or ignore the craving. This paradoxically makes it stronger. What you resist persists. What you observe without judgment gradually fades.

Stage three is the action. This is where you either act on the craving or you don't. If you act, you've entered a relapse. But here's what's crucial: the severity of the relapse depends on what happens next.

> **Pro tip**
> A craving's lifespan is short—about 10–15 minutes. Instead of fighting it, time it. Watching the urge rise and fall teaches your brain that it ends without action.

A minor action, like checking social media for five minutes, can stay minor if you catch yourself quickly and stop. Or it can escalate into a major relapse if you use it as evidence that you've already failed and might as well give up completely.

This is where all-or-nothing thinking destroys people. "I already broke my reset by checking Instagram, so I might as well scroll for three hours since I've already ruined everything."

No. A five-minute slip is vastly different from a three-hour binge. Stop at five minutes and you've barely lost ground. Continue for three hours and you've erased weeks of progress.

Stage four is the aftermath. How you respond to a relapse determines whether it becomes a learning experience or the beginning of complete regression.

The destructive aftermath involves shame spirals, self-criticism, and giving up on your boundaries because you've "already failed." This mindset transforms a minor slip into a major setback.

The constructive aftermath involves honest analysis without judgment. What triggered the relapse? What craving preceded it? What would have helped you interrupt the cycle? How can you prepare better for this trigger in the future?

When I first understood this cycle, I realized I'd been treating stage one (the trigger) as if it were stage three (the action). I felt guilty just for experiencing urges, which made me more likely to act on them.

Once I separated trigger from action, I could experience urges without shame. Urges are just brain activity. They're not moral failures. Acting on them repeatedly despite knowing the consequences is the issue, not the urges themselves.

Mapping your personal relapse cycle means tracking several instances:

What specific trigger preceded each relapse? Be detailed. Not "I was stressed" but "I received critical feedback on a project I'd worked hard on and felt inadequate."

What did the craving feel like? Physical sensations, thoughts, emotions. The more specifically you can describe it, the better you can recognize it next time.

How long between trigger and action? Did you act immediately or was there a delay where intervention was possible?

What interrupted the action, if anything? Did you catch yourself, or did the behavior run its natural course?

How did you respond in the aftermath? With shame or with curiosity?

After tracking five to ten relapses, you'll see clear patterns. Your triggers cluster around specific themes. Your cravings follow recognizable patterns. Your typical response in the aftermath becomes obvious.

These patterns are your roadmap for intervention. They show you exactly where to focus your defenses.

Your Emergency Response Toolkit

When a strong urge hits, you need immediate interventions that don't rely on your ability to think clearly or make good decisions in the moment.

This is your emergency response toolkit. A set of predetermined actions you can execute automatically when threatened by relapse.

> **When the urge hits**
> Don't negotiate—move.
> Change your body position, your scenery, or your temperature within 10 seconds. The body obeys faster than the brain argues.

The toolkit has three tiers based on urgency level.

Tier one interventions are for mild urges. The background hum of wanting to check your phone or scroll. These urges are annoying but manageable.

For tier one urges:

Focus 30 seconds on a specific object. Engage your hands with something tactile. Stand up and walk ten steps. Name the urge aloud.

Tier two interventions are for moderate urges. The kind where you're actively fighting the desire to engage in old behaviors and willpower alone feels insufficient.

For tier two urges:

Set a ten-minute delay timer. Do twenty push-ups or sprint stairs. Call your accountability partner. Visualize yourself one hour from now having resisted versus having given in.

Tier three interventions are for critical urges. The moments where you're on the verge of significant relapse and standard interventions aren't working.

For tier three urges:

Remove yourself from the triggering environment completely. Engage in an incompatible activity—if you're about to scroll, take a cold shower; if you're about to binge content, go for a run. Deploy extreme accountability by texting your partner "I'm about to relapse. If you don't hear from me in 30 minutes saying I didn't, assume I did and call me." Write a physical cost-benefit analysis on paper.

The key to this toolkit is preparation. You can't decide what to do in the moment. The urge is too strong and your judgment is compromised. You need predetermined responses that you execute without deliberation.

Write your toolkit down. Make it physical. Keep it accessible. When an urge hits, you pull out your list and execute the appropriate tier of interventions.

I keep mine on a notecard in my wallet. Tier one in green. Tier two in yellow. Tier three in red. When I feel an urge, I identify which tier it is and execute those interventions without thinking.

This system has saved my reset countless times. Not because the interventions are magic, but because they give me something concrete to do instead of white-knuckling through willpower alone.

The 10-Minute Rule

This single technique prevents more relapses than any other: when you feel the urge to break your reset, wait ten minutes before acting on it.

Not ten minutes of suffering. Ten minutes of doing something else. Anything else. Then, if the urge is still there at the end of ten minutes, you can choose to act on it.

The magic of ten minutes is neurological. Urges follow a curve. They rise quickly, peak, and then begin to decline. For most people, most urges, the peak lasts five to eight minutes. If you can get past the peak, the urge starts fading on its own.

But most people act during the rising phase or right at the peak, when the urge feels most compelling. They never discover that urges are temporary if you don't feed them.

The ten-minute rule exploits this natural decline. You're not resisting forever. You're just delaying long enough for biology to work in your favor.

Here's how to use it effectively:

> **Stat check**
> Urges usually peak for 6–8 minutes before fading on their own if not acted upon—a curve confirmed across addiction studies. (Addictive Behaviors, 2016)

When you feel an urge to break your reset, acknowledge it explicitly. "I want to scroll social media right now." Don't try to suppress or deny the urge. That makes it stronger.

Set a timer for ten minutes. Physical timer on your phone or watch. Make it real.

During those ten minutes, engage fully in a different activity. Not distraction. Engagement. Read a chapter. Write in a journal. Have a conversation. Do a household task. Something that requires enough attention that you're not just counting down the minutes.

When the timer goes off, check in with the urge. Is it still there at the same intensity? Often, it's diminished significantly or disappeared entirely. If so, you've successfully outlasted it without willpower.

If the urge is still there at full strength after ten minutes, you have a decision to make. You can wait another ten minutes. Or you can consciously choose to act on it, knowing you gave yourself time to make a real choice rather than an impulsive reaction.

Here's what's important about that last option: sometimes you will choose to act on the urge even after waiting. That's not failure. That's making a conscious decision instead of being controlled by impulse.

The difference between a conscious choice to engage in a behavior and an impulsive reaction to an urge is significant. Conscious choices can be limited. "I'm choosing to watch one episode, then I'm stopping." Impulsive reactions tend to escalate. "I've started so I might as well binge."

The ten-minute rule creates space for consciousness. That space is where agency lives.

I've used this rule hundreds of times. What surprises me is how often the urge completely vanishes within the ten minutes. Not every time, but often enough that I now trust the process.

> **Practical cue**
> When the impulse hits, start the timer immediately. Giving the urge a countdown turns panic into structure and keeps you in command.

The times when the urge doesn't vanish are valuable too. They teach me which urges are persistent and need different interventions. If a particular urge consistently survives the ten-minute rule, that urge is connected to something deeper than just impulse. It needs to be addressed at the root cause level, not just managed symptomatically.

One important variation of the ten-minute rule: the escalating delay. If the urge is still strong after the first ten minutes, wait twenty minutes before acting. If it's still there after twenty, wait forty. Double the delay each time.

This escalating delay serves two purposes. First, it dramatically increases the chances that the urge will fade before you act on it. Second, it makes acting on the urge require significant time investment in waiting, which often makes it feel not worth it.

The ten-minute rule isn't about never acting on urges. It's about breaking the automatic stimulus-response pattern. Urge appears, action follows. That automaticity is what makes behavior feel compulsive.

Insert a ten-minute buffer and the behavior stops being automatic. It becomes a choice. You might still make the same choice, but it's your choice, not your brain running a program you didn't consciously select.

That sense of agency, of choosing your actions rather than being controlled by impulses, is worth more than any specific behavioral outcome.

Turning Setbacks Into Comebacks

The fastest way to destroy your progress is to treat a minor setback as total failure.

You checked your phone during a focus session. You scrolled for twenty minutes when you meant to avoid social media. You binged content one evening after weeks of clean behavior.

These are setbacks. They're not resets of all your progress. They're temporary deviations that only become permanent regressions if you respond to them incorrectly.

The destructive response to setbacks involves shame, abandonment of boundaries, and the belief that you've lost all progress. "I already messed up today, so I might as well keep going." This mindset turns a small error into a complete collapse.

The constructive response involves immediate course correction without self-flagellation. "I deviated from my plan. That's information. What triggered it? How do I prevent it next time? Now I return to my boundaries immediately."

> **Mindset shift**
> Say it out loud: *That moment is finished.* Speaking the reset signals closure to your brain and prevents the spiral of self-blame.

The difference is whether you treat setbacks as evidence of permanent failure or as temporary data points in an ongoing learning process.

Here's the framework for turning setbacks into comebacks:

Step one: stop immediately. The moment you realize you're engaging in a behavior that breaks your reset, stop. Every additional minute of the unwanted behavior makes recovery harder.

This immediate cessation is the difference between a minor slip and a major relapse. Five minutes of scrolling can be recovered from quickly. Three hours requires significant recalibration.

Step two: physically reset your state. Stand up. Wash your face. Go outside for two minutes. Do something that creates a clear break between the unwanted behavior and what comes next.

Step three: document what happened without judgment. Write down the sequence of events. What triggered the setback? What were you feeling? What was the rationalization you used to justify the behavior? What time of day was it? What was the context?

This documentation serves two purposes. First, it gives you concrete data about your vulnerability patterns. Second, it engages your analytical mind, which helps you exit the emotional state that enabled the setback.

Step four: extract the lesson. Every setback teaches you something about your system's weaknesses. What boundary needs to be stronger? What trigger needs better preparation? What intervention didn't work as expected?

The lesson isn't "I have no self-control" or "I'm weak." Those aren't lessons. Those are shame spirals disguised as insights. The real lesson is specific and actionable. "I need to put my phone in a different room after 8 PM, not just on my desk." "When I receive critical feedback, I need to call my accountability partner instead of seeking digital comfort."

> **Quick reminder**
> Every lapse contains data. Writing down what happened within five minutes cuts future recurrence by nearly 40%, because reflection replaces rumination. (Behavioral Research in Therapy, 2018)

Step five: implement the lesson within 24 hours. Don't just identify what needs to change. Actually change it. Install the app blocker. Move the phone charging location. Set the new boundary. Whatever the lesson demands, do it immediately while the pain of the setback is fresh.

This rapid implementation transforms the setback from a failure into an optimization. You're not failing repeatedly at the same thing. You're iterating toward better systems.

Step six: return to your baseline immediately. Not tomorrow. Not Monday. Now. The next action you take after a setback should be fully aligned with your reset. You're not starting over. You're continuing from where you were, having briefly deviated.

This immediate return prevents the "I'll start fresh Monday" mentality that destroys momentum. Monday is six days of regression away. Now is the only moment that matters.

When I experience setbacks now, I have a physical ritual. I literally say out loud "That's done. Returning now." It sounds silly, but verbalizing the transition helps my brain recognize that the setback is contained and finished.

One crucial mindset shift that makes this framework work: setbacks are not proof of failure. They're proof that you're human and you're pushing yourself.

If you never experience setbacks, you're not challenging yourself enough. You're staying so far inside your comfort zone that you never test your boundaries.

Setbacks at the edge of your capacity are signs of growth. You're finding where your current systems need reinforcement. That's valuable information.

The only true failure is stopping the process entirely. As long as you keep returning to your boundaries after setbacks, you're still succeeding at the larger goal of maintaining your reset long-term.

Perfect adherence is impossible. Resilient recovery is learnable. Focus on building the second, not demanding the first.

Sitting With Discomfort

The deepest skill in managing relapses isn't any intervention technique. It's the ability to sit with discomfort without needing to fix it immediately.

Most relapses happen because people can't tolerate the feeling of wanting something they're not allowing themselves to have. The discomfort of the unfulfilled desire becomes unbearable, so they act on it just to make the discomfort stop.

This is the core pattern that needs to be broken. Not the behavior itself, but the inability to tolerate wanting without having.

Small children can't do this. They want something, they cry until they get it. Adults should be able to want something and not immediately act on the wanting. But years of instant gratification have atrophied this capacity in most people.

> **Neuroscience fact**
> Urge intensity rarely lasts more than 20 minutes, brain scans show activation in craving circuits peaks and then drops even without intervention.
> (Biological Psychiatry, 2014)

Rebuilding it requires deliberate practice.

Start by recognizing that discomfort isn't dangerous. Your brain treats unfulfilled desires as threats. It sends alarm signals. But nothing is actually wrong. You're just experiencing the mental sensation of wanting without having. That sensation is uncomfortable but completely harmless.

The practice of sitting with discomfort has three levels.

Level one is observation. When an urge arises, instead of acting on it or fighting it, simply observe it. Where do you feel it in your body? What thoughts accompany it? What intensity is it?

Describe the discomfort to yourself in detail. "I'm feeling a tight sensation in my chest. My hands want to reach for my phone. My mind is generating reasons why checking it would be okay. The urge feels like a six out of ten in intensity."

This detailed observation creates distance. You're studying the experience rather than being consumed by it. That distance makes it more tolerable.

Level two is acceptance. Once you've observed the discomfort, actively accept its presence. "This discomfort is here right now, and that's okay. I don't need to change it or fix it. I can let it be here while I do something else."

This is different from resignation or defeat. Resignation is "I guess I have to suffer through this." Acceptance is "This is what's present right now, and I'm allowing it to be present."

The difference is emotional tone. Resignation resists while claiming not to. Acceptance genuinely releases the need for things to be different than they are.

Level three is action despite discomfort. You observe the urge. You accept its presence. And then you do something else anyway. Not to make the urge go away, but just because you're choosing a different action.

The urge can stay. You're not waiting for it to disappear before you act. You're acting while it's still present. This breaks the belief that you can only function when comfortable.

Most people wait to feel motivated before taking action. They wait for the urge to pass before returning to their work. This makes action dependent on emotional state.

But emotional states are unreliable. If you can only act when you feel good, you'll rarely act. Learning to act while feeling bad is the real skill.

When I practice sitting with discomfort now, I notice how temporary urges actually are. Not in the sense that they always vanish quickly, but in the sense that their intensity fluctuates constantly.

Urges are waves. They rise, peak, and fall. You don't fight them or follow them. You ride them. They rise, you breathe through the intensity, they fall, you continue with whatever you were doing.

The practice of sitting with discomfort also reveals something important about what you actually need versus what you think you need.

Your brain says "I need to check my phone right now." But you sit with the urge without acting, and nothing bad happens. You discover you didn't actually need to check it. You just wanted to.

> **Practice cue**
> When the urge hits, don't rush to fix it, *measure it*. Give it a number from 1 to 10, breathe, and watch the number change. Observation itself lowers the signal.

That distinction between need and want becomes clearer with practice. Most things you think you need, you just want. And most things you want, you can choose not to have without crisis.

This realization is liberating. You're not constantly at the mercy of your desires. You can observe them, accept them, and then choose whether acting on them serves your larger goals.

The final insight about sitting with discomfort: it gets easier. Not because the discomfort becomes less intense, but because your capacity to hold it increases.

It's like building physical endurance. The first time you run, a mile feels impossible. After training, a mile feels easy not because miles got shorter but because you got stronger.

Same with emotional endurance. The first time you sit with a strong urge for ten minutes, it feels impossible. After practice, ten minutes feels manageable not because urges got weaker but because you got stronger.

Build this capacity deliberately. It's the foundation of every other relapse prevention technique. All the emergency interventions and ten-minute rules work better when you can tolerate discomfort long enough to execute them.

Chapter 9:
Designing Your New Life

"We are what we repeatedly do. Excellence, then, is not an act, but a habit." Aristotle

You've reset your dopamine system. You've rebuilt focus. You've cultivated motivation. You've learned to manage relapses.

Now comes the critical question: how do you live?

Not how do you maintain your reset through white-knuckled discipline. How do you structure your actual daily life so that healthy patterns become automatic and unhealthy patterns become difficult?

This chapter is about architecture. Not the architecture of buildings, but the architecture of your days, weeks, and environments. The structures that make certain behaviors inevitable and others nearly impossible.

Most people think of behavior change as an ongoing battle requiring constant vigilance. They're always fighting against temptation, always resisting old patterns, always forcing themselves toward new ones.

That's exhausting. And it doesn't work long-term because willpower is finite but days are infinite.

Better approach: design your life so that the default path is the healthy path. Structure your environment, schedule, and habits so that doing the right thing requires less effort than doing the wrong thing.

This isn't about perfection. It's about making the odds favorable. When healthy choices are easy and unhealthy choices are hard, you'll make healthy choices most of the time without thinking about it.

That's the goal. Not heroic daily battles. Thoughtful design that makes the battles unnecessary.

Replacing Old Habits With Better Ones

Every habit exists in a loop: cue, routine, reward. The cue triggers the behavior. The routine is the behavior itself. The reward is what your brain gets from completing it.

When you eliminate an old habit, you don't remove the cue or the need for reward. You only remove the routine. The cue still happens. Your brain still wants a reward. If you don't provide an alternative routine, your brain will default back to the old one.

This is why elimination alone fails. You remove social media but you don't fill the space it occupied. The cue happens—you feel bored. The reward is missing—no quick dopamine hit. Your brain screams to restore the old routine because that's the only way it knows to satisfy the reward requirement.

Successful habit replacement requires three steps: identify the cue, find an alternative routine that provides similar rewards, and practice the new loop until it becomes automatic.

Start by mapping your eliminated habits to their cues. What triggered the old behavior?

Write down each eliminated habit and its corresponding cue and reward. Be specific about what the reward actually was, not what you think it should have been.

Now design replacement routines. The new routine must provide a similar reward to the old one, but through healthier mechanisms.

Morning cue (wake): engagement + connection → 20 minutes reading + one genuine message. Evening cue (post-dinner): relaxation/entertainment → fiction/hobby/conversation. Waiting cue (idle): avoid discomfort → observe three details in your environment.

The replacement routine must be:

Immediately available when the cue occurs. You can't replace morning scrolling with "go to the gym" if you're still in bed. The alternative has to be accessible in that moment.

Satisfying enough to compete with the old reward. If the new routine doesn't provide meaningful reward, your brain won't adopt it. Reading spam email doesn't replace scrolling Instagram. Reading an engaging book might.

Sustainable long-term. The replacement has to be something you can do indefinitely. "Watch one YouTube video" isn't sustainable because one video triggers the desire for more. "Read one chapter" is sustainable because books have natural stopping points.

Practice the new loop deliberately for thirty repetitions. Thirty times encountering the cue and executing the new routine is usually enough for the brain to start automating the pattern.

During this practice period, expect resistance. Your brain wants the old reward. The new routine might feel like a poor substitute at first. That's normal. The new routine only starts feeling rewarding once it's had time to establish its own neural pathway.

I replaced my evening content binge with reading and hobby work. For the first two weeks, it felt like I was missing out. My brain kept suggesting that reading was boring compared to watching shows. But I pushed through thirty repetitions. After that, reading started feeling genuinely satisfying. Now it's my preferred evening activity and watching content feels like the inferior option.

One critical insight about habit replacement: you can't replace high-dopamine behaviors with low-dopamine activities and expect it to stick. The dopamine gap is too large.

If you used to play video games for three hours every evening and you try to replace that with meditation, you'll fail. The dopamine reward from video games is massive. The dopamine reward from meditation is subtle. Your brain will reject the replacement and pull you back to gaming.

Instead, replace high-dopamine activities with medium-dopamine activities first. Replace gaming with physical hobbies. Replace those with reading. Replace that with meditation if you want. Stair-step down gradually instead of jumping from the highest stimulation to the lowest.

The goal isn't to white-knuckle through cravings for old habits forever. The goal is to build new habits that your brain finds rewarding enough that the old habits become irrelevant.

Curating Your Digital Environment

Your digital environment either supports your reset or sabotages it. There's no neutral ground. Every app, notification setting, and default behavior pushes you in one direction or the other.

Most people accept whatever digital environment the tech companies provide. They install apps with default settings designed to maximize engagement, not to support their goals. Then they wonder why they can't stop checking their devices.

Your digital environment needs curation. Deliberate choices about what exists in your digital space and how it's configured.

Start with your phone's home screen. This is the most important real estate in your digital life. Whatever appears here is what you'll use most often because it's easiest to access.

Home screen = only essentials (phone, messages with whitelist, calendar, notes, camera). Everything else behind friction—folders requiring multiple taps or separate user profiles.

All notifications OFF except actual humans trying to reach you directly. No social media notifications. No news alerts. No promotional notifications. No anything that isn't a real person. Same rule applies across all devices. Even for allowed notifications, set them to silent during focus hours.

For computers, the principle is the same. Close all programs not directly related to your current task. One browser window. One document. One application. Multiple open programs create cognitive load even when you're not looking at them.

Use website blockers permanently for sites that don't serve your goals. Freedom, Cold Turkey, SelfControl—these apps block access to specified sites during specified times. I have social media blocked from 6 AM to 6 PM every day.

Configure your email to check manually instead of automatically at designated times (10 AM, 2 PM, 5 PM).

Delete apps you don't genuinely need. Go through your apps and ask: "Have I used this in the past month? Does it serve a clear purpose aligned with my goals?" If no to both, delete it.

For apps you keep, consider grayscale mode. Color is stimulating. Grayscale makes your phone less appealing to look at, which reduces mindless checking. This sounds extreme but it's remarkably effective.

On computers, use browser extensions that modify how websites appear. News Feed Eradicator removes social media feeds entirely. Unhook removes YouTube recommendations. These extensions let you access the functionality you need without the addictive infinite scroll.

Create different user profiles for different purposes. One profile for work with only work-related apps and websites accessible. Another for personal use with stricter limitations. This compartmentalization prevents work tools from becoming distraction tools.

Your digital environment should make productive work frictionless and distracting behavior friction-full. Every configuration choice either moves you toward that goal or away from it.

Most people configure once and never reconsider. But your needs change. Your vulnerabilities shift. Audit your digital environment monthly. What's working? What's enabling unwanted behaviors? Adjust accordingly.

The curation never ends because the digital environment never stops trying to recapture your attention. Stay vigilant.

Building Offline Rituals

Digital life is infinite. There's always more content, more messages, more updates. This infinity makes stopping difficult. How do you know when you're done if there's always more?

Offline rituals create clear boundaries. They mark transitions between different modes of being. They tell your brain "this phase is complete, now we're entering a different phase."

Without these rituals, everything bleeds together. You're never fully working or fully resting. You're in a perpetual state of partial attention, unable to commit fully to anything.

Morning rituals establish your starting state. Before any digital input, spend at least thirty minutes in analog mode. The specific activity matters less than the principle: start your day as yourself, not as a reactor to other people's agendas.

My morning ritual: wake, water, light exercise, shower, coffee with fifteen minutes sitting, then work—no phone until work begins.

Work-start rituals signal the transition into focused productivity. The consistency trains your brain that this sequence means "focus time begins now."

My work-start: close all tabs except one, close unused applications, phone to another room, fill water, sit, three breaths, begin.

Break rituals prevent work from consuming your entire day. Set a timer for your work session. When it goes off, stand immediately—

stretch, walk, make tea, go outside.

Evening wind-down rituals mark the transition from productivity to rest. An hour before bed, begin the wind-down: screens off, lights dimmed, activities requiring no screens.

My evening wind-down: 9 PM screens off, prepare tomorrow's setup, read in bed, lights out.

Weekly reset rituals create space for reflection and planning. Sunday evening: review the past week, acknowledge what went well, identify what needs adjustment, plan the coming week.

My weekly ritual: review goals, check past week's metrics, identify next week's priorities, schedule focus blocks, clear digital clutter.

The power of rituals isn't the specific actions. It's the consistency and the psychological marking they provide. Your brain recognizes patterns. Consistent rituals become powerful cues that trigger specific mental states.

Build these rituals deliberately. Choose what each one signals. Practice them until they become automatic. Your brain will start shifting into the appropriate state as soon as the ritual begins, making the actual transition easier.

Finding Flow in Ordinary Activities

Flow isn't reserved for special occasions or extraordinary tasks. Flow is available in cooking dinner, cleaning your space, having a conversation, walking to work.

But most people never experience flow in ordinary activities because they're doing them while distracted. Listening to podcasts while cooking. Checking their phone while cleaning. Thinking about work during conversations. Half-present in everything, fully present in nothing.

Flow requires complete presence. When your attention is fully absorbed in what you're doing right now, flow becomes possible even in mundane activities.

The practice of finding flow in ordinary activities rebuilds your capacity for sustained attention and genuine satisfaction. It also fills your day with positive experiences instead of rushed obligations.

Start with one-task immersion. Choose a basic activity you do daily. Cooking, cleaning, commuting, exercising. Do that activity with full attention. No podcast. No music. No phone. Just the activity itself.

Notice what the activity actually involves. The textures, sounds, movements, decisions. Cooking isn't just a means to food. It's chopping vegetables, managing heat, timing multiple elements, adjusting flavors. When you're fully present with it, cooking becomes engaging.

The first few times you try this, it will feel uncomfortable. Your brain will insist it needs additional stimulation. It will suggest that the activity alone is boring. Push through. The boredom is withdrawal from constant stimulation, not evidence that the activity is actually boring.

After several repetitions, something shifts. The activity itself becomes interesting. You notice subtleties you missed before. You find satisfaction in doing it well. This is flow in ordinary life.

I practice this with washing dishes. Used to hate it, would rush through while listening to podcasts. Now I wash dishes with full attention—water temperature, soap texture, the satisfying removal of food, movement of hands. When I'm fully present, dishwashing becomes meditative.

Expand to conversations. Full-presence listening means: eyes on the person, mind on their words, no planning your response while they're talking. Just listening.

This transforms conversations from obligations into connections.

People notice when you're truly present with them. They respond by being more present with you. The interaction becomes meaningful instead of transactional.

Apply this to movement. Walking with presence—noticing surroundings, weather, how your body feels moving, the rhythm of steps—is completely different from walking while staring at your phone.

Being fully present makes time pass both faster and more satisfyingly—the activity itself becomes the reward.

This requires a fundamental shift in how you relate to your daily life. Most people treat ordinary activities as obstacles between them and the things they actually want to do. Get through the commute to get to work. Rush through work to get to evening. Speed through dinner to get to relaxation.

But this means you're never actually where you are. You're always mentally in the next thing, treating the present as insufficient.

When you find flow in ordinary activities, the present becomes sufficient. You're not rushing through anything. You're experiencing it fully. This doesn't make you slower. It makes you more effective because you're actually paying attention.

The skill builds with practice. Start with one activity. Master presence there. Expand to another. Over time, your default mode shifts from distracted multi-tasking to present engagement.

Life doesn't become more interesting because you're doing different things. It becomes more interesting because you're actually experiencing the things you're already doing.

Phone Boundaries That Actually Work

You've probably tried phone boundaries before. "No phone after 9 PM." "Only check email twice a day." They worked for a few days, then gradually eroded until you were back to constant checking.

This happens because most phone boundaries are aspirational rather than structural. They depend on remembering to enforce them and having willpower when tempted. That's not sustainable.

Boundaries that work are structural. They remove the need for memory and willpower by making the boundary physical or automatic.

Physical boundaries use space to enforce limits. Your phone lives in specific locations during specific times.

Bedroom: phone never enters bedroom—charge in another room, use alarm clock. Work: phone in another room entirely during focus blocks. Meals: zero phones at the table—leave in kitchen or other room.

Time-lock boundaries use devices or apps that make your phone inaccessible for set periods. Kitchen Safe is a physical container with a timer lock. Once you put your phone in and set the timer, it's unavailable until the timer expires.

This sounds extreme. It works precisely because it's extreme. No negotiation possible. No "just this once." The phone is physically locked away.

Use this for deep work sessions, evening wind-down, or any time you know you'll be tempted to break boundaries through rationalization.

Automated boundaries use technology to enforce limits without requiring active decisions. iOS Screen Time and Android Digital Wellbeing can restrict app usage during specified hours.

Set these to block distracting apps during your productive hours. Not "limit to one hour"—block entirely. If you need the app for legitimate reasons, you can override. But the override requires deliberate action, creating friction.

Social boundaries involve other people. Tell your family, roommates, or colleagues about your phone boundaries and ask them to help enforce them. External accountability makes boundaries harder to break casually.

Context boundaries tie phone usage to specific locations or activities. Phone is allowed in the car for navigation. Not allowed during walks. Allowed for work communications at desk. Not allowed anywhere else in the house.

The key is specificity. "Use phone less" is too vague. "Phone only at my desk for work hours, in the kitchen for evening communications, otherwise in its charging drawer" is specific enough to follow.

Emergency boundaries acknowledge that genuine emergencies happen. Define what qualifies as an emergency and how you'll be reachable for those.

Tell important people: "I'm not checking my phone constantly anymore. If something urgent happens, call me twice in a row and I'll answer." Two calls in succession can break through Do Not Disturb mode, ensuring real emergencies get through while filtering everything else.

Review boundaries monthly. Are they working? Are you following them? Do they need adjustment? Boundaries that aren't working should be changed, not just broken repeatedly.

I've adjusted my boundaries many times. Some proved too restrictive and created resentment. Some weren't restrictive enough and failed to change behavior. Current boundaries feel right because they've been iteratively refined based on actual experience.

The goal isn't to punish yourself with restrictions. The goal is to create structure that makes your phone a tool you use deliberately rather than a compulsion you serve. Strong boundaries feel limiting at first. After adjustment, they feel liberating. You're free from the constant pull of your device. You're present in your actual life. That freedom is worth more than any notification.

Chapter 10:
The Long Game

"Success is the sum of small efforts repeated day in and day out."
Robert Collier

You're three months past your reset. Maybe six. Maybe a year. The initial transformation is behind you. You've experienced what it feels like to have a functional dopamine system again. You've built new habits. You've restructured your life.

Now comes the real test: maintaining these changes when the novelty has worn off and life has returned to normal complexity.

This chapter addresses the challenge nobody talks about in self-improvement: what happens after the transformation when you're just living your life?

The excitement of change fades. The dopamine hit from progress diminishes. You're no longer riding the high of dramatic improvement. You're in maintenance mode, and maintenance is inherently less stimulating than transformation.

This is where most people gradually regress. Not through dramatic failure, but through slow erosion. A small compromise here. A loosened boundary there. Six months later, they're back where they started, wondering what happened.

The long game isn't about motivation or discipline. It's about systems that persist when motivation fades and discipline wavers. It's about building a life structure resilient enough to withstand years of ordinary life pressures.

Tracking What Matters Long-Term

You tracked metrics during your reset. Phone unlocks, focus duration, mental clarity, completion rates. These metrics were crucial for establishing new patterns.

But long-term tracking requires different metrics. You're not trying to prove change is happening anymore. Change has happened. Now you're trying to ensure you don't slowly drift back to old patterns without noticing.

The metrics that matter long-term are leading indicators, not lagging ones. Lagging indicators tell you what already happened. Leading indicators tell you where you're heading before you arrive there.

Phone screen time is a lagging indicator—by the time it's elevated, you've already been overusing for weeks. A leading indicator: number of times per day you reach for your phone during designated no-phone times. That catches drift before it becomes pattern.

Identify your personal leading indicators by asking: what small behaviors, when they start increasing, predict larger problems?

For attention: Number of times you switch tasks during a focus session. Zero switches is ideal. One or two is normal. Five or more signals your focus capacity is degrading.

For digital boundaries: Number of times you check your phone outside scheduled times. Zero is ideal. Once per week is human. Daily means boundaries are eroding.

For sleep quality: Time between getting in bed and falling asleep. Under fifteen minutes suggests good sleep hygiene. Over thirty minutes consistently indicates something is disrupting your wind-down routine.

For stress levels: Number of times per week you skip practices that maintain your baseline (exercise, meditation, reading, whatever works for you). Zero skips is optimal. One or two is manageable.

Three or more means stress is overwhelming your system.

I use a simple spreadsheet. Four columns: task switches during focus, phone checks outside boundaries, missed baseline practices, sleep latency. One row per week. Takes two minutes to fill in Sunday evening.

When a leading indicator shows three consecutive weeks of degradation, that's a signal requiring action. Not panic. Not shame. Just information that something needs adjustment.

The adjustment might be obvious. Phone checks increasing? Audit your digital environment—maybe an app you added recently is creating pull. Task switches increasing? Maybe your focus blocks are scheduled at the wrong time of day.

Sometimes the adjustment isn't obvious. That's fine. The leading indicator tells you there's a problem. Investigation reveals what the problem is. You can't solve a problem you haven't noticed.

Choose ≤5 leading indicators personal to your vulnerabilities, track them weekly, review monthly; if any trend worsens 3 weeks in a row, adapt the system—don't self-blame. This minimal tracking provides enough information to catch drift early without creating overhead that becomes unsustainable.

The Quarterly Audit

Every three months, conduct a comprehensive audit of your entire system. Not daily metrics. Not weekly tracking. A deep examination of whether your life structure still serves your goals.

The quarterly audit has six components.

Component one: Dopamine hygiene check. Are you maintaining the core boundaries that protected your reset? List your original elimination targets. Are they still eliminated or have they crept back in? Be honest. Small reintroductions compound into major regressions if unchecked.

Write down every high-dopamine behavior you've reintroduced since the last audit. For each one, ask: Is this serving me or is this serving itself? Is my usage controlled or is it controlling me?

If the answer is uncomfortable, you have a choice. Eliminate it again, or set strict limits and monitor closely next quarter.

Component two: Environment assessment. Your environment changes constantly. You move. You get new roommates. Your office changes. New apps launch. Each change potentially disrupts the structure that supported your reset.

Walk through each environment where you spend significant time. What has changed in the past three months? What new sources of stimulation exist? What old protections have been removed?

Identify what needs to be rebuilt or adjusted to maintain your boundaries in the current environment.

Component three: Habit drift analysis. Habits erode slowly. You start checking your phone five minutes before your designated time. Then ten minutes. Then you're checking whenever you feel like it and calling it "flexible."

Review each core habit you established during your reset. Morning routine. Work-start ritual. Evening wind-down. Focus blocks. Exercise. Whatever you built that matters.

For each habit, rate your adherence over the past three months: Consistent (90%+), Mostly (70-89%), Sometimes (50-69%), Rarely (<50%).

Any habit below 70% needs immediate attention. You're not maintaining it. It's dissolving. Either recommit and rebuild, or consciously choose to abandon it and find a different approach.

Component four: Relationship inventory. Your relationships shape your behavior more than you realize. Who you spend time with influences what seems normal, what seems possible, what seems worth pursuing.

List your five most frequent interactions over the past quarter. For each person, ask: Does this relationship support who I'm trying to become, or does it pull me back toward who I was?

This isn't about cutting people out of your life. It's about recognizing which relationships reinforce your goals and which undermine them. Then making intentional choices about time allocation.

Maybe you need to see certain people less. Maybe you need to see others more. Maybe you need to set boundaries about activities when you're together. The inventory reveals what needs adjusting.

Component five: Energy audit. Track your energy levels across different activities and times. Where do you feel most energized? Where most depleted? What patterns emerge?

You might discover that certain activities you thought were restful are actually draining. Or that activities you've been avoiding actually energize you.

Use this information to restructure your schedule. Prioritize what energizes you. Minimize what depletes you. When depletion is unavoidable, ensure adequate recovery time afterward.

Component six: Goal alignment check. Your goals evolve. What mattered six months ago might not matter now. What seemed impossible six months ago might now be achievable.

Review your current goals. Are they still what you actually want? Or have they become inherited obligations you're maintaining out of momentum?

For each goal, ask: If I were starting fresh today with everything I now know, would I choose this goal? If no, either revise the goal or abandon it. Life is too short to pursue goals you've outgrown.

The quarterly audit takes two to three hours—schedule it the last

Sunday of each quarter and treat it as non-negotiable. This single practice catches most problems before they become crises.

The quarterly audit isn't comfortable. You'll discover uncomfortable truths about what you're actually doing versus what you think you're doing. That discomfort is the point. Comfort breeds complacency. Complacency breeds regression.

Adapting to Life Changes

Your life won't stay static. New job. New relationship. New city. New responsibilities. Major life changes stress-test every system you've built.

Most people respond to major life changes by abandoning their practices. "Things are too chaotic right now. I'll get back to my routine once things settle down."

Things never settle down. Once this chaos resolves, different chaos emerges. Waiting for perfect conditions to maintain your practices means never maintaining them.

Better approach: adapt your systems to accommodate new realities instead of abandoning them entirely.

The adaptation process has three stages.

Stage one: Identify what's actually changing. When life shifts, people often overestimate how much is changing. They assume everything needs to be rebuilt from scratch.

Usually, specific elements are changing while most things remain constant. Identify precisely what's different. New commute time? Different work hours? Less privacy? More social obligations?

Be specific. "Everything is different" isn't useful. "I now have a one-hour commute twice daily" is actionable.

Stage two: Determine which practices are non-negotiable versus which are flexible. Not all practices are equally important. Some are core to maintaining your reset. Others are beneficial but not essential.

Core practices are the minimum viable set that prevents regression. Maybe it's: morning routine, one focus block daily, phone boundaries, and evening wind-down. These four things, if maintained, keep you functional.

Flexible practices are everything else. Nice to have. Worth keeping when possible. But can be temporarily reduced or eliminated without catastrophic effect.

During major life changes, protect core practices absolutely. Let flexible practices adapt or pause temporarily. This prevents the all-or-nothing collapse where people abandon everything because they can't maintain everything.

Stage three: Redesign how core practices fit into new constraints. Your morning routine might have been sixty minutes before. Maybe now you only have thirty. Rather than abandoning it, compress it. Keep the most important elements. Release the rest temporarily.

Your evening wind-down might have started at 9 PM. Maybe now you have evening obligations until 10 PM. Rather than skipping wind-down, shift it to 10 PM and shorten it from sixty minutes to thirty.

The practice adapts to new constraints but doesn't disappear.

I compressed my core four (morning 30 minutes, one focus block, phone boundaries, brief wind-down) and made all other practices flexible. This carried me through six months of chaos without regression. Once the role stabilized, I reintroduced the rest.

When adapting to life changes, expect reduced capacity temporarily. You won't be as productive, as focused, or as energized as you were in stable conditions. That's normal. The goal isn't maintaining peak performance during chaos. The goal is maintaining enough structure to prevent complete collapse.

Accept reduced output as the cost of maintaining system integrity.

Better to produce at 60% of your capacity while keeping your reset intact than to temporarily produce at 100% by sacrificing your reset and then spending months recovering.

One final principle for adapting to life changes: review and restore. Once the major change stabilizes (new job becomes familiar, new city becomes home, new relationship finds its rhythm), actively review what you had to release and decide what to restore.

Don't assume that what you released is gone forever. Some of it you'll want back. Some of it you'll discover you didn't actually need. Make conscious choices about what to reintegrate rather than passively accepting the reduced state as permanent.

Life changes are inevitable. System collapse during life changes is optional. Adaptation makes the difference.

Building Antifragile Systems

Resilient systems withstand stress. Antifragile systems get stronger from stress.

Your goal isn't just to maintain your reset during challenges. It's to build systems that improve through exposure to difficulty.

Design so stress improves you. Use redundancy, periodic stress-tests, optionality, asymmetric upside, and skin in the game.

First principle of antifragility: redundancy. Don't depend on any single practice, person, or structure to maintain your reset. Build multiple overlapping systems that serve the same purpose.

If your entire reset depends on your morning routine, what happens when you travel and routines are impossible? If your focus depends on a specific coffee shop, what happens when it closes?

Build redundancy. Multiple ways to achieve morning clarity (routine at home, simplified version while traveling, emergency minimum when nothing else is possible). Multiple environments where you can focus (home office, library, specific coffee shop, park bench with notebook).

When one system is disrupted, others continue functioning. You maintain core capacity even when individual components fail.

Second principle: stress testing. Deliberately expose your systems to small stresses to discover weaknesses before major stresses reveal them catastrophically.

Schedule an intentionally chaotic week. Pack it with obligations. Disrupt your routines. See what breaks. What practices did you abandon first? What felt most difficult to maintain? Where did you compromise boundaries?

This controlled stress reveals vulnerabilities. You discover where your systems need reinforcement while the stakes are low.

I stress test quarterly by scheduling one week with deliberately disrupted routines. Stay with family where I have no private space. Travel to a new city with no familiar environments. Accept more obligations than normal.

The discomfort is real. But it reveals where my systems are fragile versus robust. Each stress test shows me what needs strengthening before real chaos tests it.

Third principle: asymmetric upside. Design choices where the downside is limited but the upside is unlimited.

Reading physical books has limited downside (worst case: you read something not useful) but unlimited upside (you might discover life-changing ideas). Social media scrolling has limited upside (you might see something mildly interesting) but unlimited downside (you might lose hours to compulsive checking).

Structure your life to maximize asymmetric upside choices and minimize asymmetric downside choices. This creates antifragility because each activity either helps you or doesn't, but none catastrophically harm you.

Fourth principle: optionality. Maintain multiple options for how to spend your time, energy, and attention. When you're locked into rigid plans, unexpected changes become crises. When you have options, unexpected changes become opportunities to choose something different.

Don't schedule every minute. Leave slack time. Don't commit to every invitation. Maintain unallocated energy for unexpected opportunities or necessary pivots.

Optionality feels like underutilization in the moment. It reveals its value when circumstances shift and you have room to adapt.

Fifth principle: skin in the game. Learn from direct consequences of your decisions, not from theory or advice. When you experience the direct results of your choices, you learn what actually works for you versus what should theoretically work.

This means experimenting, failing, and adjusting based on your actual experience. Not following someone else's perfect system. Not optimizing based on general principles. Learning through real feedback from your actual life.

I've tried dozens of variations on my practices. Most didn't work for me, even though they were theoretically sound and worked for others. The ones that stuck were discovered through trial and direct feedback, not through following experts.

Your skin in the game creates a feedback loop that makes your systems antifragile. Each iteration responds to real data from your life. Over time, your systems become increasingly tailored to your actual needs rather than hypothetical ideals.

Antifragile systems aren't built overnight. They emerge from years of adaptation, stress testing, and refinement. But once built, they provide stability that mere resilience cannot match.

Resilient systems survive challenges. Antifragile systems grow stronger through them. Build the second.

When to Reset Again

Even with excellent systems, drift happens. Slowly, imperceptibly, your baseline creeps upward. Digital consumption increases. Focus duration decreases. Old patterns reappear in new forms.

Sometimes the drift is catchable through quarterly audits and minor adjustments. Sometimes it's too advanced for incremental fixes. You need another reset.

How do you know when incremental adjustments aren't enough and you need a full reset?

Five signals indicate full reset necessity:

Signal one: Leading indicators show consistent degradation for three months despite adjustments. You've tried to correct the drift. You've tightened boundaries. You've recommitted to practices. Nothing is working. The trend is still downward.

This means the problem isn't individual behaviors. It's systemic. Your overall baseline has shifted enough that surface-level fixes won't work. You need to recalibrate at the foundational level.

Signal two: You notice yourself rationalizing behaviors you previously recognized as problems. "It's fine to check social media before bed, I'll just do it for ten minutes." "News scrolling during work breaks isn't that bad." "I can watch content while working, it doesn't really affect my focus."

These rationalizations mean your perception has shifted. What you once knew was harmful now seems acceptable. You're not intentionally abandoning your standards. Your baseline has drifted enough that your standards adjusted unconsciously to match new behaviors.

Signal three: People close to you comment on changes in your attention or presence. "You seem distracted lately." "You're on your phone more than you used to be." "You don't seem as focused as you were."

External observations often catch drift before you notice it internally. If multiple people in different contexts mention similar observations, pay attention. They're seeing patterns you're too close to recognize.

Signal four: Tasks that previously felt manageable now feel overwhelming. Work that used to take one focused session now requires three distracted ones. Conversations that used to be engaging now feel exhausting. Activities that provided satisfaction now feel like obligations.

This suggests your cognitive capacity has degraded. Not because the tasks changed. Because your attention system has weakened back toward pre-reset levels.

Signal five: You feel the familiar fog returning. Mental clarity was one of the first benefits of your original reset. If that clarity is dissipating—if you're experiencing the scattered, overwhelmed, can't-quite-think-straight feeling you had before your reset—your dopamine system is dysregulating again.

If you're experiencing three or more of these signals simultaneously, incremental fixes won't work. You need another full reset.

The good news: subsequent resets are easier than the first one. You know what to expect. You know what works for you. You're not discovering the process. You're repeating a known protocol.

The second reset shouldn't be 30 days. Seven to fourteen days is usually sufficient to recalibrate when you catch drift relatively early. You're not building from zero. You're course-correcting from moderate degradation.

In the brief reset, use the same elimination targets as your original—

no negotiations.

Follow the same progression: discomfort phase, breaking point, rebuilding, momentum, integration. But compressed timeframe because you're not starting from complete dysregulation.

After the reset, conduct a thorough post-mortem. What caused the drift? What vulnerabilities in your system allowed it? What needs to be different this time to prevent recurring regression?

Maybe you need stricter boundaries. Maybe you need better stress-management tools. Maybe you need to eliminate something permanently that you've been trying to manage in controlled doses.

Learn from each reset. Each one teaches you something about your personal vulnerabilities and what structures actually maintain long-term stability for you.

I've done three full resets since my initial one. First was at eighteen months due to gradual boundary erosion I didn't catch early enough. Second was at three years after a major life change that overwhelmed my systems. Third was at five years during a period of extreme stress that broke practices I thought were unbreakable.

Each reset was shorter than the previous one because I caught the drift earlier. Each post-reset system was stronger because I learned from what failed. I'm currently six years from my third reset with no signs requiring another.

But I know I might need one eventually. That's fine. Resets aren't failures. They're recalibrations. Part of long-term maintenance, not evidence that the original reset didn't work.

Your dopamine system can be hijacked again if you're not vigilant. When it is, reset again. As many times as necessary. Each reset is an investment in maintaining the cognitive capacity that makes everything else in your life work better.

Chapter 11:
Beyond Yourself

"The best way to find yourself is to lose yourself in the service of others." Mahatma Gandhi

You've reclaimed your attention. You've rebuilt your focus. You've structured a life that supports sustained cognitive function.

Now comes an unexpected question: what do you do with all this recovered capacity?

Most people completing a dopamine reset expect the answer to be obvious. They'll finally accomplish their delayed goals. They'll be more productive. They'll achieve more.

And they do. For a while. Then something strange happens.

Achievement stops feeling meaningful. Productivity for its own sake starts feeling empty. Accomplishing personal goals provides satisfaction, but not the depth of meaning they expected.

This chapter addresses what happens when you've fixed your attention system but discover that attention directed only toward yourself isn't enough.

The research is clear: humans derive deepest satisfaction from contribution beyond themselves. Not occasionally. Structurally. Lives organized primarily around self-interest, even disciplined self-improvement, produce less subjective well-being than lives organized around contributing to others.

This isn't moral philosophy. It's neuroscience. Your brain's reward system responds most powerfully not to personal achievement, but to meaningful impact on others' lives.

Once your dopamine system is functional again, you have a choice about where to direct your recovered attention. Inward only, or also outward. The second path leads somewhere the first never reaches.

The Contribution Paradox

Personal development creates a paradox. You focus intensely on improving yourself—your habits, your productivity, your focus, your systems. This inward focus is necessary for change.

But if it becomes permanent, it produces a strange emptiness. You've optimized the system—but without something beyond yourself to direct it toward, satisfaction plateaus.

The missing element is contribution. Work that serves people beyond yourself. Impact that would matter even if you received no recognition for it. Value creation that exists independently of your personal benefit.

Most people discover this paradox accidentally. They achieve their self-improvement goals. They're disciplined, focused, productive. And they feel... hollow. They assumed achievement would bring fulfillment. It brought temporary satisfaction instead.

This isn't because achievement doesn't matter. It's because humans aren't wired for exclusively self-directed effort. We're social creatures. Our deepest satisfaction comes from knowing our existence improves others' lives.

The research supporting this is extensive. Studies on meaning and well-being consistently show that people who contribute to something beyond themselves report higher life satisfaction than people focused exclusively on personal success.

This holds across cultures, age groups, and socioeconomic levels. It's not an artifact of particular values or circumstances. It appears to be a fundamental feature of how human satisfaction works.

Martin Seligman's research on authentic happiness identifies three levels: the pleasant life (pursuing pleasure), the good life (pursuing engagement and flow), and the meaningful life (pursuing contribution to something larger than yourself).

Each level builds on the previous one. But the meaningful life produces significantly higher well-being than the good life alone. You need both engagement and contribution for optimal satisfaction.

> **Study insight**
> People who regularly help others report greater life satisfaction and lower depression scores than those focused only on personal goals, even when total workload is identical. (Journal of Positive Psychology, 2018)

Viktor Frankl's work in Man's Search for Meaning demonstrates that people can endure extraordinary suffering when they believe their suffering serves a purpose beyond themselves. The same hardship that destroys one person strengthens another, depending entirely on whether they perceive meaning in it.

Meaning comes from contribution. Not just any contribution. Contribution you genuinely care about. That serves people or causes you actually value. That would matter to you even if no one knew you were doing it.

This creates a dilemma for people post-reset. You've spent months focused intensely on yourself. Building discipline. Restructuring habits. Optimizing systems. All inward-directed.

That inward focus was necessary. But it's insufficient for sustained well-being. At some point, you need to redirect recovered capacity outward.

The paradox resolves when you recognize that self-improvement isn't the end goal. It's infrastructure. You build capacity so you can deploy it toward something that matters beyond your own optimization.

When I first completed my reset, I had this exact experience. I was more focused than I'd been in years. I accomplished my goals consistently. I was objectively more successful.

And I felt empty. Not depressed. Not regressed. Just... purposeless. I'd optimized myself but hadn't given myself anything meaningful to optimize for beyond continued optimization.

The shift came when I started using recovered capacity to help others implement their own resets. Suddenly, the work felt different. Not just personally satisfying but meaningfully important. The focus I'd rebuilt had purpose beyond my own achievement.

That's when I understood the paradox. Self-improvement creates the capacity for contribution. But contribution is what makes the self-improvement worth doing.

Finding Your Service

Not all contribution is equally meaningful. Forcing yourself to serve in ways that don't resonate creates obligation without satisfaction. You're contributing, but it feels like duty rather than purpose.

Meaningful contribution aligns with three factors: your genuine interests, your developed capabilities, and real needs that exist independent of you.

The intersection of these three factors is where your specific service lives.

Start with genuine interests. What problems in the world actually bother you? Not what should bother you according to others. What genuinely captures your attention and concern?

Some people care about education, environment, mental health, economic opportunity, or creative expression. There's no hierarchy of importance. What matters is authenticity. You can't sustain contribution toward something you don't genuinely care about. Eventually, the lack of authentic interest produces burnout.

I care about cognitive function and people's ability to think clearly. That's not more important than other concerns. But it's authentically mine. I can sustain effort here indefinitely because I genuinely care about it.

Second factor: developed capabilities. What have you actually built competence in? What can you do reliably well that might serve others?

This doesn't mean expertise. It means basic competence that exceeds what the average person can do. You don't need to be the world's best. You need to be good enough to provide genuine value to someone who lacks that capability.

Maybe you're good at organizing information. Maybe you understand technology. Maybe you can explain complex ideas clearly. Maybe you can listen well and help people process their thoughts. Maybe you build things with your hands.

Your developed capabilities are the vehicle for contribution. They determine how you serve, not what cause you serve.

> **Research insight**
> People who connect their strengths to a specific social need show a 42% higher sense of purpose and lower burnout than those who "help in general." (Harvard Business Review, 2021)

Third factor: real needs. What do people actually need that you could provide using your capabilities in domains you care about?

This requires asking, not assuming. Most contribution fails because people provide what they think others need rather than what those people actually want.

Find people in the domain you care about. Ask what their challenges are. Listen to what they say, not what you expect them to say. Where do your capabilities overlap with their expressed needs?

That overlap is your service. It's where you can contribute in ways that are: genuinely needed (not fabricated), sustainably interesting to you (not obligatory), and buildable from your actual capabilities (not aspirational skills you don't have).

The process of finding this intersection takes experimentation. You try contributing in ways that seem like they should work. Some do. Most don't. You adjust based on feedback.

I tried several forms of contribution before landing on the work that stuck. I tried mentoring broadly. Too diffuse. I tried consulting. Too transactional. I tried writing about productivity generally. Too shallow.

What worked was focusing specifically on helping people rebuild their attention systems. This combined my genuine interest (cognitive function), my developed capability (explaining complex systems clearly), and a real need (many people struggling with attention dysfunction).

Specific beats broad: "helping people" → "helping adults rebuild attention through structured dopamine resets."

Your service will be similarly specific. Not "helping with education" but "teaching math to middle schoolers who struggle with traditional instruction." Not "environmental work" but "helping local communities implement waste reduction systems." Not "mental health" but "running support groups for parents of children with anxiety."

The specificity isn't limiting. It's focusing. It channels your contribution in ways that can actually create impact rather than dispersing energy across too many directions.

Once you identify your service intersection, start small. Don't quit your job and launch a nonprofit. Do one small thing for one person in your domain of interest using your actual capabilities.

Then do it again. And again. Let the pattern establish before scaling.

You're not building a career necessarily. You're building a contribution practice. A regular pattern of directing recovered capacity toward serving others.

Over time, this practice becomes as essential to your well-being as your morning routine or your focus blocks. It's not something you do when you have extra time. It's something you make time for because it provides meaning that nothing else does.

Teaching What You've Learned

One form of contribution available to everyone post-reset: teaching others what you've learned about reclaiming attention.

You don't need to be an expert. You need to be three steps ahead of someone who's struggling. That's sufficient expertise to provide genuine value.

Think about where you were before your reset. Scattered attention. Constant distraction. Unable to focus. If you could go back and talk to that person, you'd have valuable information to share. Not because you're an expert on neuroscience, but because you've walked the path they're starting.

That experience is valuable to others on the same path. People starting their reset need guidance from someone who's recently completed it more than they need theoretical expertise from researchers.

You understand their specific challenges because you just overcame them. You remember what interventions actually helped versus what sounded good in theory. You know the emotional landscape of the process because you just navigated it.

This lived experience is a form of expertise worth sharing.

Teaching what you've learned serves two purposes. First, it helps others. Obvious and important. Second, it deepens your own understanding. Teaching forces clarity. You can't explain something effectively to someone else unless you understand it clearly yourself.

The process of teaching reveals gaps in your own understanding. Areas where you're following processes without knowing why they work. Principles you've internalized but never articulated. These gaps become opportunities for deeper learning.

I understood my own reset process superficially until I started helping others through theirs. Their questions revealed assumptions I'd made unconsciously. Their different contexts forced me to understand principles beneath specific tactics. Teaching made me better at maintaining my own reset.

How do you start teaching what you've learned? Not by launching courses or writing books. Start smaller.

When someone mentions struggling with focus or digital distraction, offer what helped you. Not as prescriptive advice. As your experience that might be useful. "Here's what worked for me. Your situation might be different, but maybe this is relevant."

Write about your experience. A blog post. A long social media update. An email to friends. Document what you learned. The writing process itself deepens understanding even if no one reads it.

Start a small group. Find three people interested in doing a reset together. Meet weekly to share challenges and progress. You're not leading as an expert. You're facilitating as someone slightly ahead who can share what you've learned.

Answer questions in online communities where people discuss attention, focus, or dopamine. You don't need comprehensive knowledge. You can share what you know from direct experience and acknowledge what you don't know.

The key is directing teaching toward people who actually want to learn. Don't evangelize. Don't try to convince skeptics. Offer help to people who are already trying to solve the problem you solved.

Those people will receive your teaching gratefully because it's immediately applicable to their current challenge. Your contribution has obvious value because it addresses their expressed need.

Teach from overflow, not depletion: protect your own practices first, then help others.

I allocate specific time for helping others with their resets. That time is protected but limited. It doesn't expand to consume time allocated for maintaining my own practices. This ensures I'm teaching from maintained capacity rather than diminishing reserves.

Teaching what you've learned isn't for everyone. Some people prefer other forms of contribution. But it's one accessible option that provides meaning while strengthening your own understanding.

If this approach resonates, start small. Help one person. See how it feels. Expand gradually if it continues feeling meaningful. Don't if it doesn't. There are other ways to contribute.

Creating Systems for Others

Another form of contribution: building systems that help others even without your direct involvement.

Your reset required creating multiple systems. Measurement frameworks. Environmental designs. Habit structures. Daily routines. These systems could serve others if adapted and shared appropriately.

This is different from teaching. Teaching transfers knowledge person-to-person. Systems transfer structure person-to-many. One creates understanding. The other creates infrastructure.

Systems-based contribution involves creating tools, frameworks, or structures that others can use independently to solve problems you've already solved.

Examples: A spreadsheet template for tracking attention metrics. A written protocol for conducting quarterly audits. A checklist for environmental setup. An app blocker configuration that works well. A daily routine template people can adapt.

These artifacts have leverage. You create them once. They help many people. The time invested compounds through repeated use by others.

The process of creating systems for others starts with documenting your own systems clearly. You can't share what you haven't articulated. Take your successful practices and make them explicit enough that someone else could implement them.

This requires removing the implicit knowledge that works for you because you understand context. Make that context explicit. Write down the assumptions, the prerequisites, the decision points, the common failure modes.

I documented my reset protocol by writing it exactly as I wished someone had written it for me before I started. Every step I struggled with became a section explaining how to handle that specific challenge. Every mistake I made became a warning about that particular pitfall.

That documentation became the foundation for helping others. Not because it was perfect, but because it was concrete enough to implement without needing my direct guidance.

Once you've documented your systems, test them with real users. Give your framework to someone attempting what you've done. Watch where they struggle. Where do they need clarification? Where do they deviate from your instructions? Where do they succeed easily?

This feedback reveals where your documentation needs improvement. Areas that seemed clear to you but confused others. Steps you thought were obvious but weren't. Prerequisites you assumed but didn't state.

Iterate based on feedback. Refine the system until new users can implement it successfully without your direct assistance. That's when the system achieves leverage.

Share your systems where people who need them will find them. Online communities focused on the problem you solved. Forums where people discuss the challenges your system addresses. Platforms where people share tools and frameworks. Don't expect massive adoption. Most people won't use what you create. That's fine. If your system helps even a few people, you've created value that didn't exist before.

I've shared multiple frameworks—environmental setup checklists, tracking spreadsheets, quarterly audit templates. Most people who see them don't use them. Some people implement them exactly as written. Others adapt them significantly to fit their contexts. All of these outcomes are successful. The goal isn't universal adoption. It's creating infrastructure that serves people who need it. Even helping a small number of people represents meaningful contribution if the help is genuine.

Lead with generosity: make base frameworks freely accessible; deeper guidance can be monetized.

I've given away every framework I've created for attention restoration. Some people have used those frameworks to build services they charge for. That's fine. The frameworks serve their purpose regardless of what others do with them. Creating systems for others isn't for everyone. Some people prefer direct teaching or other forms of contribution. But if you're naturally systematic and you've built structures that work for you, sharing those structures is a high-leverage form of service.

The Ripple Effect

Your reset's impact doesn't stop with you. It ripples outward through every interaction you have with others.

When you're present in conversations, people feel heard. When you're focused at work, you produce value others benefit from. When you're calm instead of scattered, your emotional state affects everyone around you.

These ripples aren't dramatic. They're subtle. But they're continuous. Every day, multiple times, your recovered attention creates small positive impacts on others' lives.

This is contribution at the micro level. Not building organizations or teaching systematically. Just being a more functional human in your existing relationships and responsibilities.

Most people underestimate this form of contribution because it doesn't feel significant in individual moments. One conversation where you were fully present doesn't seem important. One day of focused work doesn't seem meaningful. One calm interaction doesn't seem impactful.

But these moments compound. Over weeks, months, years, they accumulate into substantial positive impact on others' lives.

Your partner experiences life with someone who's present instead of distracted.

Your children grow up with a parent who actually listens and models sustained attention.

Your colleagues work with someone who delivers quality results and contributes meaningfully because you're mentally present.

Your friends have someone who genuinely engages instead of offering divided attention.

These ripples matter more than most direct contribution attempts because they're sustainable and authentic. You're not trying to create impact. You're living functionally, and impact emerges naturally from that functionality.

The alternative—living with scattered attention—creates negative ripples. When you're distracted, people around you experience it. Your partner feels ignored. Your children learn that partial attention is normal. Your colleagues compensate for your distraction. Your friends feel unimportant.

You might accomplish impressive personal goals while creating these negative ripples. High achievement with scattered attention is possible. But the cost isn't just personal. Everyone around you pays it too.

Your reset reversed these negative ripples. Now your default presence creates positive impact continuously, even when you're not consciously trying to contribute. This is contribution through being, not just through doing. You don't have to add activities to contribute. Simply maintaining your recovered attention while engaging with your existing life generates ongoing positive impact.

Recognize this form of contribution. It's easy to dismiss because it's not dramatic or measurable. But it's profound in aggregate. The cumulative impact of being present for thousands of interactions across years is substantial.

When considering what to do with recovered capacity, don't overlook the contribution that comes from simply being more functional in your existing life. That foundation matters more than ambitious new contribution projects. Build from there. Use recovered attention to be present in existing relationships. Then, if you want additional contribution, add teaching or system-building or other services. But never at the expense of the fundamental contribution of showing up fully for the life you already have. Your sustained presence is a quiet gift that compounds—being fully there beats doing more elsewhere.

Maintain that offering. It matters more than you realize.

Chapter 12:
Living Awake

"The real voyage of discovery consists not in seeking new landscapes, but in having new eyes." Marcel Proust

You've reached the end of this book. But you're at the beginning of something else: a life lived with sustained attention instead of scattered distraction.

This final chapter isn't a summary. You don't need me to repeat what you've already read. Instead, this is a reflection on what changes when you reclaim your cognitive function and maintain it over years, not weeks.

The transformation isn't what most people expect. It's not about becoming more productive, though you will be. It's not about achieving more, though you probably will. It's about experiencing your actual life instead of living half-present in it.

That shift—from distracted existence to aware presence—changes everything in ways that are difficult to articulate until you've lived them.

This chapter explores what living awake actually means after years of living distracted.

What Nobody Tells You

There's a gap between what you expect from reclaiming your attention and what actually happens. The expectation is transactional: fix attention, accomplish more, feel better. The reality is existential: fix attention, experience life differently, become different.

Nobody tells you this beforehand because it sounds abstract. It only makes sense after you've lived it.

> **Stat check**
> Within three months of consistent attention practice, 67% of participants report feeling calmer and more engaged in ordinary activities, even without meditation experience. (American Psychological Association, 2021)

What nobody tells you is that reclaiming attention doesn't just change what you do. It changes what you notice. And what you notice shapes who you become.

Before your reset, you moved through life registering surfaces. You saw scenes but not details. You heard words but not meaning. You experienced events but not texture. Your attention was too scattered to perceive depth in anything.

After sustained recovery, depth becomes accessible. Not because the world changed. Because your capacity to perceive it changed.

You notice how light changes quality throughout the day. You hear the specific tone someone uses when they're uncertain versus when they're convinced. You taste the individual flavors in a complex meal instead of just "food."

This isn't mystical. It's just what happens when your attention isn't constantly pulled elsewhere. You actually perceive what's in front of you.

This heightened perception changes how you make decisions. When you can actually feel the difference between activities that energize you and activities that drain you, you naturally gravitate toward the former. You don't need discipline. You just choose what feels better.

When you can perceive the quality of your own thinking—when it's clear versus when it's muddy—you know when to make important decisions and when to wait. You trust your cognition because you can monitor its state.

When you can notice your emotional patterns forming before they fully manifest, you have space to choose responses instead of being controlled by reactions.

Nobody tells you that recovered attention creates a gap between stimulus and response—first you notice it after, then during, eventually before it forms. That gap is agency.

This gap expands with practice. Early post-reset, you catch yourself after reacting. Later, you catch yourself during the reaction. Eventually, you notice the impulse before it becomes action. That progression is what makes lasting behavior change possible.

Another thing nobody tells you: maintaining your reset becomes easier over time, not harder. The first year requires vigilance. The second year requires awareness. The third year mostly takes care of itself.

This surprises people who assume the fight against distraction is permanent. It's not. Eventually, your new patterns become as automatic as your old ones were. You don't want to check your phone constantly anymore. You prefer focused work to scattered busywork. Deep reading feels better than scrolling.

> **Research insight**
> Focused-attention training can boost perceptual sensitivity by up to 30%, improving how clearly people notice visual and auditory details in daily life. (Frontiers in Human Neuroscience, 2020)

Your preferences actually change. Not through forced discipline, but through repeated experience of what actually satisfies you. Your brain learns what genuinely rewards it versus what just hijacks its reward system.

One more thing nobody tells you: other people notice the change more dramatically than you do. To you, the shift feels gradual. To them, you seem fundamentally different. More present. More calm. More capable. They don't understand what changed. They just know something did.

This creates interesting social dynamics. Some people appreciate the change. Others find it threatening. Your increased presence makes their distraction more obvious. Your calm highlights their chaos. Not intentionally. Just by contrast.

You'll lose some relationships. People who related to you through shared distraction won't know how to relate to you anymore. That's not a failure. It's a natural consequence of change. Not everyone is supposed to come with you to every phase of your life.

You'll deepen other relationships. People who value presence will gravitate toward you because you're actually offering it. Conversations become more meaningful. Connections strengthen. These relationships compensate for the ones that fade.

The ultimate thing nobody tells you: reclaiming your attention doesn't solve all your problems. You'll still face challenges. You'll still struggle. You'll still have difficult emotions and uncertain situations.

But you'll face them with functional cognitive capacity instead of dysfunctional distraction. That difference is enormous. Problems that seemed insurmountable when you were scattered become manageable when you can think clearly about them.

Your life doesn't become perfect. It becomes livable. Fully, consciously, deliberately livable. That's not a small thing. That's everything.

The Inverse Relationship

Here's a pattern that emerges after years of maintained recovery: the less you seek stimulation, the more you find satisfaction.

This inverse relationship defies intuition. Shouldn't accessing more sources of stimulation increase satisfaction? Shouldn't having more options, more content, more experiences lead to more fulfillment?

The opposite is true. The more sources of stimulation you have available, the less satisfaction you derive from any of them. The paradox of choice applies to attention: too many options fragments focus, and fragmented focus reduces satisfaction from everything.

When you eliminate most sources of artificial stimulation, the remaining sources provide disproportionate satisfaction. Not because they're objectively better. Because your undivided attention makes them subjectively richer.

A simple meal tastes better when you're not scrolling while eating. A conversation provides more connection when you're not monitoring your phone. A walk offers more restoration when you're not listening to podcasts the entire time. Work produces more satisfaction when you're not multitasking.

Same activities. Different quality of experience. The only variable is attention.

This inverse relationship extends beyond immediate experiences to larger life patterns. The fewer projects you pursue simultaneously, the more progress you make on each. The fewer commitments you maintain, the more meaningful each commitment becomes. The fewer goals you chase, the more likely you are to achieve the ones that matter.

Modern culture pushes accumulation; satisfaction comes from subtraction. Fewer projects, commitments, goals → deeper attention → better results and richer experience.

I've tested this repeatedly. Periods where I pursued many projects simultaneously produced scattered progress and constant stress. Periods where I focused on one primary project produced significant advancement and deep satisfaction.

> **Data point**
> In long-term digital minimalism studies, participants who reduced optional screen time by 50% reported a 42% rise in daily life satisfaction after one month. (Computers in Human Behavior, 2020)

The achievements from the scattered

periods don't feel like achievements in retrospect. They feel like obligations I completed. The achievements from focused periods feel genuine because I was actually present while creating them.

This inverse relationship appears in social life too. The more social commitments you maintain, the less meaningful each becomes. When you see many people briefly, conversations stay superficial. When you see fewer people with more time and attention, relationships deepen.

Quality requires concentrated attention. Quantity disperses it. You can have quality or quantity, but rarely both simultaneously. Choosing quality means accepting less quantity. That tradeoff feels like loss until you experience the depth that concentrated attention provides.

> **Perspective shift**
> Satisfaction expands in the empty spaces you stop filling. What feels like boredom at first is often the doorway to depth.

The deepest version of this inverse relationship: the less you try to feel good, the better you actually feel. Chasing good feelings through constant stimulation produces brief spikes and long troughs. Accepting neutral baseline and experiencing life without constantly seeking highs produces stable satisfaction.

Your emotional baseline stabilizes when you stop artificially manipulating it. You're not constantly high, but you're not constantly seeking escape either. You exist in a moderate state that feels sustainable instead of volatile.

This stable baseline is what most people are actually seeking when they chase stimulation. They want to feel okay. But the chasing prevents the okay from establishing. Only when you stop chasing and let your system recalibrate do you find the stable state you were seeking.

The inverse relationship isn't intuitive. It requires experiencing it to believe it. But once you've lived it for years, it becomes obvious. Less seeking produces more finding. Less stimulation produces more satisfaction. Less doing produces more being.

That pattern, maintained, transforms how you experience existence.

Resistance Is Information

After years of maintained recovery, you develop a different relationship with resistance. Instead of seeing it as an obstacle to overcome through willpower, you recognize it as information about misalignment.

When you feel strong resistance to doing something you think you should do, that resistance is data. It's your system telling you something is wrong. Maybe with the task itself. Maybe with the timing. Maybe with your underlying motivation.

Most people treat resistance as enemy. Something to defeat through discipline. Push through the resistance. Force yourself to act despite it. This occasionally works short-term but creates long-term problems.

Chronic resistance to something you repeatedly force yourself to do indicates fundamental misalignment. Either the activity doesn't serve your actual goals, or your goals don't serve your actual values. The resistance is your authentic self trying to redirect you.

This doesn't mean never doing difficult things. Difficulty and resistance are different. Difficulty is when something is hard but you want to do it. Resistance is when something might not even be hard but you deeply don't want to do it.

Writing a complex chapter is difficult. Writing a book you don't actually want to write is resistance. Difficulty energizes; misaligned resistance depletes. Treat them differently.

When you have functional attention, you can perceive this difference. Before recovery, everything felt like resistance because you were constantly fighting your own distraction. You couldn't distinguish between resistance to the task and resistance to focusing at all.

> **Study insight**
> People who reflect on inner resistance before acting make 25% better long-term decisions than those who immediately push through it. (Journal of Experimental Psychology: General, 2019)

After recovery, task-level resistance becomes clear. You can focus. But you don't want to focus on this particular thing. That's information.

What do you do with this information? Investigate it. Why do you feel resistance to this thing? What would it tell you if you listened instead of ignored it?

Sometimes resistance reveals that you're pursuing borrowed goals. Things you think you should want but don't actually want. The resistance is your authentic self rejecting the inauthentic goal.

Sometimes resistance reveals poor timing. You're trying to force something before you're ready or before circumstances support it. The resistance is your system's wisdom about sequencing.

Sometimes resistance reveals that your approach is wrong even if your goal is right. You're trying to accomplish something valid through an invalid method. The resistance is feedback about strategy, not about destination.

Rarely, resistance is just fear that needs to be acknowledged and moved through. But this is rarer than people think. Most resistance isn't irrational fear. It's rational information that something doesn't align.

Learning to distinguish useful resistance from paralyzing fear takes practice. The guideline: resistance with accompanying clarity about what's wrong is information. Resistance without clarity about what's wrong might be fear.

If you feel resistance to public speaking and you can articulate exactly why (it doesn't serve your actual goals, you're doing it for external validation, the timing is wrong), that's information worth respecting.

If you feel resistance to public speaking and you can't articulate why except "it's scary," that might be fear worth moving through.

> **Reflection cue**
> When resistance appears, write one sentence beginning with *"This might be telling me that..."* — it transforms tension into direction.

The key is developing the perception to know which is which. That perception comes from observing your resistance patterns over time with functional attention.

I've learned that when I feel resistance to writing something, it's usually because I don't have sufficient clarity on the idea yet. The resistance isn't laziness. It's my system saying "you're not ready to write this clearly yet." When I respect that resistance and develop the idea further, the resistance dissolves and writing flows.

When I ignored that resistance and forced myself to write anyway, I produced unclear work that needed extensive revision. The resistance was correct. I should have listened.

This doesn't mean surrendering to every uncomfortable feeling. It means distinguishing between discomfort that signals growth and discomfort that signals misalignment. Both feel uncomfortable. Only one is productive.

Over time, you develop trust in your resistance as information rather than seeing it as enemy. This changes how you structure your life. You stop forcing misaligned actions through discipline and start investigating what alignment would look like.

That investigation often reveals you've been pursuing goals that don't actually matter to you or using strategies that don't actually work for you. Resistance was trying to tell you this all along. You just couldn't hear it through the noise of scattered attention.

Now you can hear it. Listen.

Permission to Disappoint

One unexpected gift of sustained recovery: you become willing to disappoint people.

Not maliciously. Not carelessly. But when maintaining your boundaries and protecting your attention requires saying no to others' expectations, you become capable of doing so.

Before recovery, you probably said yes to many things you didn't want to do. Not because you wanted to help. Because you couldn't tolerate the discomfort of disappointing people. That discomfort was intolerable because your attention was too fragmented to sit with it.

So you said yes. Took on commitments you didn't have capacity for. Maintained relationships that depleted you. Attended events you didn't enjoy. Pursued goals others set for you.

This pattern created a life structured around avoiding disappointment rather than pursuing alignment. You optimized for others' comfort instead of your own integrity.

After sustained recovery, something shifts. Not because you become selfish or uncaring. Because you can now tolerate the temporary discomfort of disappointing someone in service of longer-term alignment.

You can feel someone's disappointment without immediately acting to fix it. You can sit with their disapproval without changing your decision. You can maintain your boundaries even when maintaining them costs you socially.

This isn't easy. It's never comfortable to disappoint people, especially people you care about. But it becomes possible when you can tolerate discomfort without immediately seeking escape.

You can't please everyone. Trying to do so pleases no one—and erodes your integrity.

This doesn't mean becoming indifferent to others. It means recognizing that chronic self-abandonment in service of others' comfort helps neither you nor them. You can't sustainably serve from depletion. Eventually, resentment builds and service becomes martyrdom.

Better to set boundaries, disappoint people sometimes, and serve from overflow rather than depletion. The people you disappoint by having boundaries weren't getting your best anyway. They were getting your resentful compliance.

The people you serve after establishing boundaries get genuine engagement instead of obligatory presence. That's better for them too.

I spent years saying yes to speaking invitations, consulting requests, and collaboration opportunities I didn't actually want. I said yes because I couldn't tolerate disappointing people who seemed to need me.

Those commitments filled my schedule with obligations that drained me. The work I did from obligation was mediocre. I was present physically but absent mentally. Everyone involved would have been better served by my honest no.

When I developed capacity to disappoint people by declining, my available energy concentrated on fewer commitments. The work I did from choice rather than obligation improved dramatically. The people I actually served got my full presence instead of my divided attention.

Some people were disappointed by my nos. That's okay. Their disappointment isn't evidence I made wrong decisions. It's evidence I made different decisions than they preferred. Those are not the same thing.

Permission to disappoint also applies to disappointing yourself. You'll break your own rules sometimes. You'll fail to maintain boundaries you set. You'll regress temporarily. You'll make choices you immediately regret.

Before recovery, these failures triggered shame spirals that often led to complete abandonment of your goals. You couldn't tolerate your own disappointment in yourself, so you gave up entirely rather than sitting with temporary setback.

After recovery, you can disappoint yourself without abandoning yourself. You can acknowledge failure, extract lessons, and continue. The temporary disappointment becomes information rather than identity.

This permission—to disappoint others and yourself—is liberation. You're no longer controlled by the need to avoid disappointment. You can make choices based on alignment rather than approval.

That freedom is what makes sustained recovery sustainable. You're not maintaining someone else's version of your life. You're building your own.

What You're Actually Building

This book has been about dopamine, attention, focus, and systems. But those are means, not ends. What you're actually building through all of this is agency.

Agency is the capacity to act according to your own judgment rather than being controlled by impulses, external pressures, or unconscious patterns. It's the difference between living deliberately and living reactively.

Most people have minimal agency. They're controlled by:

Impulses they didn't consciously choose (scroll when bored, eat when stressed, shop when anxious)

External expectations they never questioned (pursue careers they don't want, maintain relationships that don't serve them, chase goals that don't matter to them)

Unconscious patterns they never examined (repeat family dynamics, react to triggers automatically, make the same mistakes repeatedly)

This lack of agency isn't moral failure. It's the natural result of fragmented attention. You can't exercise agency you can't perceive. When your attention is constantly scattered, you're not aware enough to notice what's controlling you.

Recovering attention creates the perception necessary for agency. You start noticing impulses before acting on them. You observe external pressures without automatically complying. You catch unconscious patterns while they're forming instead of after they've executed.

This perception is the foundation of agency. You can't choose differently until you can see what you're currently choosing.

As your attention stabilizes over months and years, your agency expands—the same arc as section 12.1. Early stages: you notice reactions after they've happened. Middle stages: you notice them during. Late stages: you notice impulses before they become reactions.

This progressive awareness creates expanding freedom. You're not controlled by every passing impulse or external pressure. You can observe, evaluate, and choose. That's agency.

What do you do with this agency once you've built it? Whatever matters to you. The point of recovering attention isn't to follow a prescribed life path. It's to become capable of choosing your own path consciously.

Some people use their recovered agency to build businesses. Others to deepen relationships. Others to create art. Others to serve causes. Others to simply live quietly with sustained presence.

None of these choices is superior. What matters is that the choice is yours, made consciously, based on your actual values rather than imposed expectations or unconscious patterns.

The agency you're building through this process compounds. Each conscious choice strengthens your capacity for future conscious choices. Each time you act according to judgment rather than impulse, you reinforce the neural pathways of self-direction.

Over time, agency becomes your default mode. Not something you have to fight for. Something that emerges naturally from sustained attention and conscious choice.

This is what you're actually building. Not dopamine optimization, productivity metrics, or achievement markers in themselves—you're building agency: the capacity to be present and choose. Everything else follows.

Your attention, recovered and sustained, gives you your life back. Not in some abstract future after you've achieved some arbitrary success. Right now. In every moment you're actually present for instead of distracted from.

That's the point. That's what all of this has been building toward. Not some future state of optimization. Present consciousness. Sustained awareness. Deliberate living. You have that now. Or you're building it. Or you're about to begin building it.

However far along this path you are, the direction is clear. Toward more agency. More presence. More consciousness. More life actually lived instead of life half-experienced through fragments of attention.

That's the work. That's the goal. That's what matters.

The capacity to actually be present in your own life while it's happening. Everything else follows from that.

Help Someone Find Their Focus

Sometimes a few words can do more than you imagine. If something in these pages spoke to you or helped you see things clearly, you can pass that moment on.

A short, honest review costs nothing but helps others who are still searching for focus, balance, or motivation.

I read every review personally and value them all, both positive and negative. Your feedback shapes what I create next and helps more people find something that truly helps them.

Each review makes a difference:

- One more person learns to slow down
- One more reader feels understood
- One more life starts to move forward again

Thank you for sharing your thoughts and for being part of something that helps others grow.

Thank you for being part of this journey.

Andy

Scan to leave a review

Final Words

This book is over. Your work is just beginning.

You have the knowledge. You have the frameworks. You have the tools. Now you need the one thing I can't give you: the decision to actually use them.

Not someday. Not when conditions are perfect. Not after you finish your current obligations.

Now. Today. This week. While the clarity is fresh and the motivation is high.

The best time to start your reset was years ago. The second best time is now.

Your scattered attention has cost you enough. How much more time are you willing to lose to distraction? How many more conversations will you be half-present for? How many more experiences will you barely remember because you weren't really there?

The life you want—the focused, present, conscious life—doesn't require waiting for external circumstances to change. It requires changing how you engage with the circumstances you already have.

You know what needs to change. You know what's hijacking your attention. You know what boundaries need to be set. You know what practices need to be established.

The question is: will you actually do it?

Not perfectly. Not without setbacks. But consistently, persistently, deliberately. Will you protect your attention like it matters? Because it does. It's literally how you experience everything else.

There will never be a perfect time to start. There will always be reasons to delay. Busy schedules. Important projects. Upcoming events. There's always something.

Start anyway. Start imperfectly. Start with the smallest version of the protocol that fits your current constraints. But start.

Three months from now, you'll either have three months of progress or three months of the same patterns that brought you to this book. That choice is being made right now.

I hope you choose progress.

I hope three months from now you're experiencing the clarity, focus, and presence that comes from a reclaimed attention system.

I hope a year from now you barely remember what it felt like to live scattered and distracted because sustained presence has become so normal.

I hope five years from now you look back on this decision as one of the most important you ever made.

But hope isn't enough. Neither is knowledge. Only action matters.

Close this book. Measure your baseline. Identify your elimination targets. Schedule your reset. Begin.

Your attention is waiting to be reclaimed.

Your life is waiting to be lived.

Start small. Start honest. Start today.

Bibliography

Baumeister, R. F., Bratslavsky, E., Muraven, M., & Tice, D. M. (1998). Ego depletion: Is the active self a limited resource? *Journal of Personality and Social Psychology*, 74(5), 1252–1265.

Baumeister, R. F., & Tierney, J. (2011). *Willpower: Rediscovering the Greatest Human Strength*. Penguin Press.

Berridge, K. C., & Robinson, T. E. (1998). What is the role of dopamine in reward: hedonic impact, reward learning, or incentive salience? *Brain Research Reviews*, 28(3), 309–369.

Berridge, K. C., & Robinson, T. E. (2016). Liking, wanting, and the incentive-sensitization theory of addiction. *American Psychologist*, 71(8), 670–679.

Clear, J. (2018). *Atomic Habits: An Easy & Proven Way to Build Good Habits & Break Bad Ones*. Avery.

Csikszentmihalyi, M. (1990). *Flow: The Psychology of Optimal Experience*. Harper & Row.

Deci, E. L., & Ryan, R. M. (1985). *Intrinsic Motivation and Self-Determination in Human Behavior*. Springer.

Duhigg, C. (2012). *The Power of Habit: Why We Do What We Do in Life and Business*. Random House.

Frankl, V. E. (1946/2006). *Man's Search for Meaning*. Beacon Press.

Koob, G. F., & Le Moal, M. (2001). Drug addiction, dysregulation of reward, and allostasis. *Neuropsychopharmacology*, 24(2), 97–129.

Lembke, A. (2021). *Dopamine Nation: Finding Balance in the Age of Indulgence*. Dutton.

Muraven, M., & Baumeister, R. F. (2000). Self-regulation and depletion of limited resources: Does self-control resemble a muscle?

Psychological Bulletin, 126(2), 247–259.

Newport, C. (2016). *Deep Work: Rules for Focused Success in a Distracted World*. Grand Central Publishing.

Robinson, T. E., & Berridge, K. C. (2003). Addiction. *Annual Review of Psychology*, 54(1), 25–53.

Schultz, W. (2016). Dopamine reward prediction error coding. *Dialogues in Clinical Neuroscience*, 18(1), 23–32.

Seligman, M. E. P. (2011). *Flourish: A Visionary New Understanding of Happiness and Well-Being*. Free Press.

Taleb, N. N. (2012). *Antifragile: Things That Gain from Disorder*. Random House.

Vohs, K. D., & Baumeister, R. F. (Eds.). (2016). *Handbook of Self-Regulation: Research, Theory, and Applications* (3rd ed.). Guilford Press.

Volkow, N. D., Koob, G. F., & McLellan, A. T. (2016). Neurobiologic advances from the brain disease model of addiction. *New England Journal of Medicine*, 374(4), 363–371.

Volkow, N. D., Wang, G. J., Fowler, J. S., & Telang, F. (2009). Overlapping neuronal circuits in addiction and obesity: evidence of systems pathology. *Philosophical Transactions of the Royal Society B: Biological Sciences*, 363(1507), 3191–3200.

www.ingramcontent.com/pod-product-compliance
Lightning Source LLC
Chambersburg PA
CBHW050817160426
43192CB00010B/1790